FUR TRADE
IN CANADA

FUR TRADE IN CANADA

KEITH WILSON

FOCUS ON CANADIAN HISTORY SERIES

Grolier Limited
TORONTO

Cover: Bivouac of a Canoe Party, *painting by Frances Ann Hopkins*

Cover Design: Didier Fiszel

Maps: Jane Davie

Illustration Credits: Public Archives of Canada, cover and page 46; Ontario Ministry of Natural Resources, page 12, Hudson's Bay Company, pages 14, 19, 32, 35, 36, 41, 48, 62, 64, 67, 68, 70, 72, 73, 77 and 81; Glenbow Alberta Institute, page 25; Ontario Ministry of Industry and Tourism, page 50; Public Archives of British Columbia, page 56; Manitoba Archives, page 74.

Canadian Cataloguing in Publication Data

Wilson, Keith, 1929-
    Fur trade in Canada

(Focus on Canadian history series)
Includes index.
ISBN 0-7172-1807-4
ISBN 0-7172-1813-9 (pa.)

1. Fur trade - Canada - History. I. Title.
II. Series.

FC3207.W54   971   C80-094658-8
F1060.W54

Contents

Preface

There are many good reasons for studying history. To begin with, we need to know something of the past if we are fully to understand the present, for many of the things we do are influenced by events which happened long ago.

History, however, does more than teach us about those events; it also teaches us something about human nature and how the actions and thoughts of people reflect their surroundings and traditions. If we question why things happened and why people thought and acted as they did in the past, we can learn to understand why some people today act and think differently from each other and from us.

History is not just about wars and acts of government. History covers everything that happened in the past, and the past can be as near as yesterday. If you have ever wondered how Canada came into being, you need to learn something of the fur trade and the men and women who worked in it. The fur trade was as important to early Canada as oil is to Saudi Arabia today.

Canada has had quite an exciting history—wars, explorations, pioneering struggles, heroism, greed and self-sacrifice. As you read of the voyages of Cartier and Champlain, the explorations of La Vérendrye and Mackenzie and the ruthless efficiency of Governor Simpson of the Hudson's Bay Company, you should go back in your imagination and try to understand why these people acted as they did and what hardships they had to overcome. You may not always approve of the things they did, but you must remember that there are always at least two sides to every question.

You can probably put yourself quite easily in the place of Cartier when he first saw the Indians and traded for furs. But try also to put yourself in the place of the Indians when they first saw Cartier's ship approaching. And you must be careful not to judge the actions of people in the past by your own standards today. What seems unfair or dishonest to you may have been perfectly acceptable generations ago. Remember too that perhaps in another hundred years historians may be judging you!

Now a comment about the use of names. This is always a problem to anyone writing about the past. To be really accurate, we cannot refer to places before they existed or before they were named. We cannot say that La Vérendrye reached a certain town if at that time the town did not exist. What we really should say is that he reached a spot where a particular town now stands. Another problem arises when names change their meanings. A good example is the name *Canada*. Today, when we use it we mean all of the nation as it now exists. But Canada in 1867 covered only Nova Scotia, New Brunswick and parts of modern Ontario and Quebec. Still earlier, Canada included only parts of present-day Ontario and Quebec. To avoid confusion, names in this book are used with their present meanings.

I hope that you will enjoy this story of the fur trade and that you will be interested enough to begin looking at the history that is all around you in your own community.

I would like to thank Ken Pearson who encouraged me to write this book and Jocelyn Smyth who edited the manuscript and made many helpful suggestions.

Introduction

You have probably noticed that a Canadian five-cent coin has a beaver on one side and the Queen's head on the other. You know, of course, that the Queen is Queen of Canada, but have you ever wondered why the beaver is so honored? It is an interesting story because the beaver and other fur-bearing animals were very important in the early history of Canada.

Fur-bearing animals were always plentiful in Canada, and you can probably guess that two of the reasons for this are climate and terrain. The geography of Canada is mainly the result of the Ice Age. Millions of years ago, glaciers covered most of the North American continent. These glaciers were like enormous rivers of ice. They levelled much of the hilly land, cut hollows which later became lakes, and forced rivers to find new channels by filling their former beds. The ice had completely melted by about eleven thousand years ago, but the receding glaciers left a land with little topsoil, dotted with thousands of lakes and connecting streams. This vast area is now known as the Canadian Shield, and it stretches from Labrador to the Northwest Territories in a large arc. If you have ever travelled along the northern shores of the Great Lakes, you will have some idea of what the fringes of the Shield look like. With its countless waterways, its many wooded areas and its cold climate, it is an ideal home for many fur-bearing animals.

For centuries this land was also sparsely populated. The first inhabitants began to arrive shortly after the Ice Age. These were the ancestors of the Inuit and of the people now known as Indians. They probably came originally from Asia across the land bridge which scientists believe once spanned the Bering Strait. Gradually, over a period of thousands of years, they spread throughout the continent. As the various groups became separated, they developed different languages and adopted ways of life suited to the area in which they lived.

Most Indians became nomads, constantly moving from place to place in search of food. The animals they killed provided that food as well as clothing and shelter. While the Plains Indians lived off the vast herds of buffalo, other tribes soon learned to trap the smaller fur-bearing animals.

For several centuries after the Norsemen reached Canada about A.D. 1000, Europeans remained ignorant of the American continent. Then came John Cabot's journey to Newfoundland in 1497. It led indirectly to the beginning of the fur trade, and the fur trade attracted to the shores of Canada first the French and then the English.

For hundreds of years, the French and the English had fought wars in Europe, and they brought this rivalry with them to Canada. Each enlisted the aid of certain Indian tribes for the Indians were vital to the fur trade. They gathered most of the furs for the traders, showed them the trails and canoe routes which opened up the country, and taught them to survive in the harsh climate. The Indians gained much from their early contacts with the traders. They acquired firearms and better tools, and in some ways led an easier life. But they also paid a price for this. They suffered appallingly from diseases against which they had no resistance. They grew to depend too much on the traders, and they eventually lost many of their traditional skills.

The fur trade shaped the early history of Canada. From the French discovery of the country's fur riches, the trade grew rapidly. It spurred the exploration of half a continent, destroyed a way of life, and caused long and bitter conflicts among both Indians and Europeans. It led ultimately to the birth of a new nation stretching from coast to coast. Within the fur trade, the beaver was always dominant. It is entirely fitting, then, that in 1975 the Canadian Parliament honored the beaver as a "symbol of the sovereignty of Canada."

The Beaver

From the earliest times of prehistory, men and women have worn furs. The cavemen of northern Europe must have huddled around their meagre fires clutching crude robes of animal fur to keep out the bitter winter chill. For many hundreds of years, poor peasants used the furs of wild or domestic animals both for clothing and for shelter. But by the Middle Ages furs had found another value. Apart from keeping people warm in the cold stone castles of the time, they also became symbols of power and authority. Kings, princes and barons trimmed their robes with magnificent ermine, and many rich merchants donned other furs to show their wealth and their importance.

In the 1500s there was a great demand for all types of furs, especially the high-quality furs which only the rich could afford. The best furs came to western Europe from the cold regions of northern Russia and Scandinavia because most animals grow their thickest furs in the extremely cold climates of those countries. Among the wealthy nobles, the most popular furs for many years were ermine and marten. Those who could not afford ermine and marten bought cheaper furs to line their clothes. The furs of otter, squirrel and fox were actually less expensive than heavy wool cloth. The seamstresses preparing the wedding clothes for one French princess in the fourteenth century used 11,794 squirrel skins, all imported from Scandinavia!

During the Middle Ages a regular fur trade developed, with furs being sold at the great fairs at Leipzig and other European cities. Towards the end of the 1400s, however, supplies of the

The beaver's fur is very dense and fine, with long coarse guard hairs scattered through it. Its large hind feet are webbed for fast swimming and its broad flat tail is covered with scaly skin. Beavers are sociable and placid animals, who quickly seek safety in the water when alarmed. They warn others of danger by slapping the surface of the water with their tails.

best-quality furs were gradually running out, and people had to begin using other furs and seeking new supplies. Then, within a few decades, the main demand was for beaver. This happened because of a new fashion among the wealthier people of western Europe—the beaver hat. Hatters found that beaver fur was especially suited for making a durable felt which could be shaped in many different ways. For this they used the soft fur with numerous little barbs which remained after the long glossy guard hairs had been removed. According to some historians, however, the hatter's trade had its dangers. In the process of making felt, the hatters used a compound of mercury. As they worked, they could not avoid breathing in some of the poisonous compound.

This gradually affected their brains and gave rise to the well-known saying "mad as a hatter."

Castor Canadensis

The beaver is descended from the giant *Castoroides* which grew to 350 kilograms or more and lived about a million years ago. It is the second largest rodent in the world, the largest being the capybara, which lives in South America. Rodents are animals that gnaw, and they include rats, squirrels and gophers. Today there are only two living species of beaver: the *Castor fiber*, found in small numbers in Europe, and the *Castor canadensis*, found in North America.

The *Castor canadensis* is a large animal which, at full growth, can be up to 1.3 metres in length and weigh almost thirty kilograms. Its fur is usually dark brown and consists of a thick woolly undercoat covered by a layer of shiny guard hairs.

The beaver is ideally suited for a life spent mainly in the water. Its paddle-like tail is effective as a rudder, and its hind feet are webbed for fast swimming. It can close its ears, nostrils and mouth when submerged, and its eyes are protected from under-water debris by clear sliding shields. Near its tail are two sacs containing a yellow, oily fluid called *castor* or *castoreum*. The beavers use this to waterproof their fur, but it is also used as a base for expensive perfumes.

Beavers are vegetarians and they eat no meat of any kind. Their usual diet consists of roots of water plants, twigs and the bark of favorite trees such as the poplar, birch and willow. They depend heavily on their teeth, which grow continually, and which are as sharp as chisels. They can gnaw down trees up to a metre in diameter, and it takes them as little as three minutes to fell a willow of ten centimetres in diameter.

Beavers are also great engineers. For safety, they always stay near water. First they build a dam to halt the water flow of a stream and create a large pond. They start building the dam by putting green brush and branches into the water with the cut ends upstream. The current presses the branches into the mud of the stream bed and this gives the beaver a good foundation to which

Beavers usually make their home near the bank of a sluggish stream. In order to maintain a supply of water that will hide the entrance of their lodge and allow for food storage, they build a dam across the stream at a place below their settlement. They begin in the centre of the channel and work from there to each shore. The dam shown here was about 200 metres long and almost 2 metres high.

he adds sticks, mud and stones. Floating debris also gets caught in the dam which gradually builds up, sometimes to enormous proportions.

Once they have made a pond, the beavers build their home or lodge. They first make an island by piling up sticks and mud, and this island then becomes the floor of their lodge. Then they build a mound of mud about 60 centimetres high and use this as a temporary support for a roof, which they make by piling on sticks and covering them with earth. When the dome reaches a height of about 1.5 metres, the beavers remove the mud through underwater tunnels. This leaves them a large and safe home on a solid foundation. With their supply of food stored underwater near the tunnels, the lodge provides a secure and comfortable haven for the harsh Canadian winter.

Each spring a litter of young beavers is born in the darkness of the lodge. The new-born beavers are known as "kits," and a litter usually includes three or four. They soon learn to help their parents by cutting trees and repairing the dam and lodge. They normally stay with their parents for about two years, so that there are often as many as eight or ten beavers in one lodge. At the age of two, they leave to find their own mates and to build their own dam and lodge. Beavers always keep their own mate, and they usually live from twelve to fifteen years unless killed by their natural enemies, the otter, wolf or lynx, or by men.

It is men, who have devised many clever means of catching them, who are the deadliest of all the beavers' enemies. In the earlier days, many Indians used to smash in the domes of the beaver lodges; later traps were invented which were humane and did not damage the furs. Today, the methods of trapping vary greatly across Canada and often depend on the climate and the thickness of the ice.

It has been estimated that there were as many as ten million beavers in North America before the white man came. Nonetheless, when the demand for beaver fur was at its height, there was a very real danger that excessive trapping would wipe out the species. Changes in fashion and a growing concern for conservation have fortunately saved it from extinction, and the beaver continues to be a considerable source of wealth for Canada.

Beginnings and New France

By the year 1500, many Europeans were becoming aware for the first time of the vast continent which lay to the west and would soon be named America. European merchants had long grown wealthy by trading in spices from the Fast East, but they had problems in getting these spices quickly and cheaply. The overland route was long, dangerous and costly, so they began searching for a dependable sea route. The famous voyage of Columbus in 1492 revealed that a new continent blocked the western route to Asia. The merchants then had two alternatives: they could reach the Indies by sailing round the southern tip of Africa or by finding a route around or through the newly discovered continent of America. Thus began the search for the Northwest Passage.

In 1497 John Cabot, a Venetian sailor employed by Henry VII of England, was the first to explore Canadian waters. After more than a month at sea, he sighted land at Belle Isle and then turned south to Griquet on the northern shore of Newfoundland. There he landed, erected the banners of St. George and St. Mark, and formally took possession of the land for the English king. The discovery of snares and nets proved that the land was inhabited, but he saw no people. He then explored the jagged eastern coast-line of Newfoundland but did not land again. One reason may well have been his fear of the vicious mosquitoes which at one time were thought to be the size of chickens!

Cabot returned to England firmly convinced that he had found Asia, but he also reported having sailed through great seas of fish "which are caught not only with the net but with baskets." This news certainly kept up an interest in the area. Many fishermen from western Europe made their way to these incredibly rich fishing grounds, but they were interested only in the fish and not in exploration.

The Voyages of Cartier and the First Trading Posts

No further exploration in fact took place for over thirty years, until Jacques Cartier set sail from St. Malo, France, in 1534. He hoped to find precious metals and possibly a route to Asia. Failing that, he would claim any new lands he discovered for the French king. Sailing through the Strait of Belle Isle, Cartier explored the coast of Labrador, which was so desolate that he called it "the land God gave to Cain." He then crossed the Gulf of St. Lawrence and passed the Magdalen Islands where birds were "as thick ashore as a meadow with grass." At another little island he noticed "several big beasts, big as oxen, with two teeth in their mouths like the elephant." He had seen his first walrus! After touching the tip of Prince Edward Island, Cartier then explored the mainland coast of the Gaspé Peninsula.

There he met two fleets of Indian canoes and noted in his journal that the Indians "made frequent signs to us to come on shore, holding up to us some furs on sticks." Later, he wrote, "they sent on shore part of their people with some of their furs; and the two parties traded together. They bartered all they had to such an extent that all went back naked without anything on them; and they made signs to us that they would return on the morrow with more furs." This was the beginning of the fur trade in Canada.

At first the trade in furs did not grow very rapidly. Most of the visitors to this region still came for fish; nearly every year, fishermen from Spain, Portugal, France and England crossed the Atlantic to the rich cod-fishing grounds of the Grand Banks off Newfoundland. As they landed to dry their catch and mend their nets, however, they met the local Indians, who willingly traded furs for implements and other small articles. This trade gradually increased, and before many years had passed, regular trading posts were established every summer. The main post was at Tadoussac, where the Saguenay River enters the St. Lawrence.

As the sixteenth century drew to a close, the fur trade began to surpass fishing in value. Then, as beaver hats became fashionable in Europe, the fur trade in the Saguenay region grew even more quickly. The Indians organized a more efficient trapping system, and they also developed a method of treating beaver furs which made them especially valuable to the European traders with whom they dealt.

Many Indians in this cold northerly region used beaver fur for clothing. They took the pelts in winter when they were of prime quality. They then scraped the inner sides, rubbed them with animal marrow and cut them into rectangles for stitching together as robes. They wore these robes with the fur next to the body, and with wearing, the long guard hairs fell out and the fur became soft and ideally suited for making felt. These furs were later known as *castor gras d'hiver* (greasy winter beaver). The furs which had not been worn were called *castor sec* and were less valuable.

Early Settlement and Exploration

As the trade increased, the French naturally thought of strengthening their position by setting up a permanent trading post. Cartier had tried to do this at Stadacona (now Quebec) in 1541, but he had found the difficulties too great. The Indians were hostile, and many of the settlers could not face the hardships of a Canadian winter. The settlement was soon abandoned and no new attempt was made for almost sixty years.

In 1600 a small group of French merchants again tried to set up a permanent post at Tadoussac. Although it lasted only a year, they did not give up. In 1603 they sent two ships to trade in furs and to explore the St. Lawrence more thoroughly. On board one of the ships was Samuel de Champlain, the man destined to become the founder of French Canada.

Champlain was already an experienced seaman. He had journeyed to the West Indies where he had seen the rich Spanish colonies and he now wanted to judge whether Canada would be a suitable colony for France. At Tadoussac he met a band of Algonquins who now controlled the traffic in furs down the Ottawa

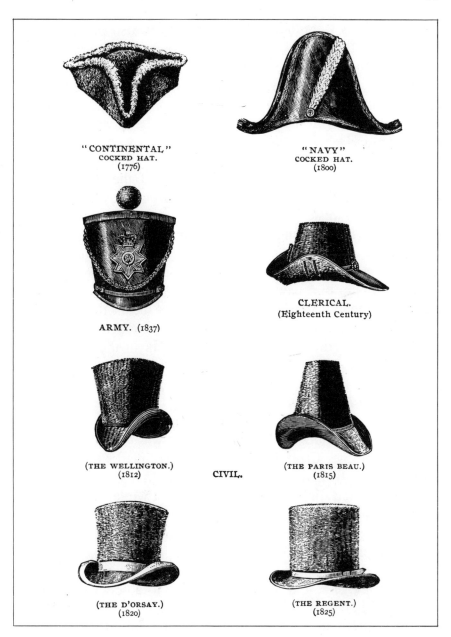

"CONTINENTAL"
COCKED HAT.
(1776)

"NAVY"
COCKED HAT.
(1800)

ARMY. (1837)

CLERICAL.
(Eighteenth Century)

(THE WELLINGTON.)
(1812)

CIVIL.

(THE PARIS BEAU.)
(1815)

(THE D'ORSAY.)
(1820)

(THE REGENT.)
(1825)

In the early seventeenth century, the demand for pelts created by the popularity of beaver hats spurred efforts to establish permanent trading posts in what is now Canada. Two centuries later, the beaver hat was as popular as ever among gentlemen, members of the clergy and army and navy officers.

River. Not only were they eager to trade, they also wanted French help against their tribal enemies, the Iroquois. While they, and the Montagnais in the Saguenay area, were willing to let the French settle, they wisely did not encourage French exploration inland. This might have put the French in direct touch with the fur-hunting tribes in the interior and would have weakened their own control. The Algonquins and Montagnais were shrewd businessmen, determined to keep their trading advantages and profits.

Champlain, impressed by the riches of the fur trade and convinced that the South Sea (Pacific Ocean) lay only a little farther to the west, gave a favorable report on his return to France. The French king then took immediate steps to establish a permanent colony. He commissioned a nobleman, the Sieur de Monts, to establish a settlement and convert the Indians to Christianity. To help him pay the costs of this, the King granted him a ten-year monopoly of the fur trade. This meant that de Monts could control the trade and fix prices high enough to make the money he needed. Among his collaborators in the project was Champlain.

The Acadian Experiment

Like Cartier, De Monts found that building a settlement was more difficult than he thought. The first attempt was on an island at the mouth of the Ste. Croix River, which today marks the boundary between New Brunswick and the state of Maine. The colonists were ill prepared for the horrors of their first winter. Their shelter was inadequate and the winter so cold that "the cider froze in the casks and each man was given his portion by weight." They ran short of fuel, food and fresh water, and an outbreak of scurvy caused the death of thirty-six men. In the spring survivors wisely decided to move across the Bay of Fundy to a better site, which they called Port Royal.

At Port Royal, Champlain directed the building of a "habitation" with a well-protected and spacious warehouse, living quarters, mill and even a garden. During their first winter there, Indians came from near and far to bring them fresh meat and to barter beaver and otter skins. Life was now far more bearable,

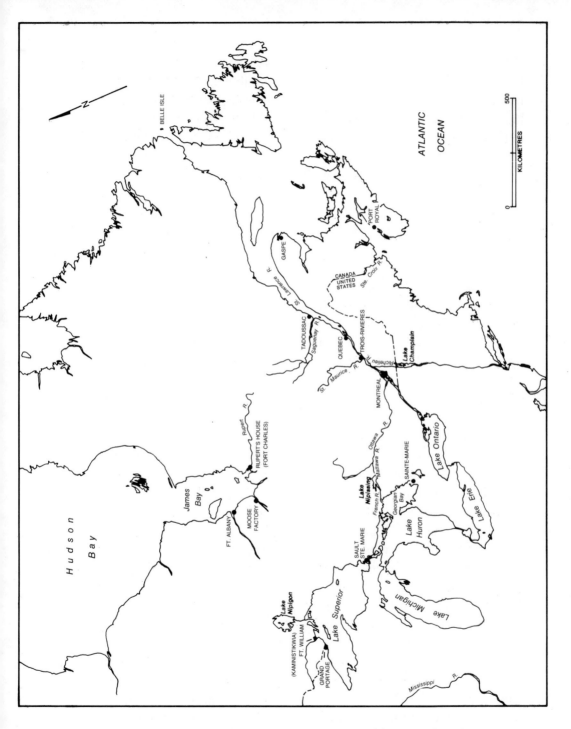

The main waterways, settlements and trading posts of eastern Canada.

and to keep their spirits high, Champlain organized the Order of Good Cheer. Every two weeks, one member of the small community took his turn at providing an evening's food and entertainment for the others. Each tried to outdo the one who had gone before, and the resulting feasting and merriment helped carry them through the winter.

But Port Royal was not well situated for controlling the fur trade, and the habitation was temporarily abandoned in 1607. Then, in the following year, Champlain established a fur-trading post at Quebec which became the first permanent settlement in New France.

The Founding of Quebec

Quebec was an ideal site. Champlain clearly saw the importance of this natural rock fortress which commanded the narrow part of the St. Lawrence River. He called it Quebec from the Indian word *kebec* meaning "a narrowing of waters." Immediately he began to strengthen it by building a habitation, and in less than a month his men had erected three frame houses around a courtyard in which stood a watchtower. Strong walls protected this cluster of buildings, and outside them all ran a moat on three sides and the river on the fourth. With cannon commanding the river approaches, it was well defended against any attack.

The founding of Quebec was perhaps Champlain's greatest achievement, and it had many important results. Because of its permanence and its location, it gave Frenchmen a strong and well-organized base from which to control the trade, stop the unlicensed 'free traders,' and begin explorations to the interior. It also gave them a much-needed feeling of security. The fledgling colony at Quebec nevertheless faced many problems. At first, of course, it was simply a small trading post and fort, and its garrison suffered terribly during the first winter. Only eight people survived the bitter cold, the scurvy and the dysentery to greet the arrival of the supply ship in the spring. With the coming of the first true settlers, Louis Hébert and his family, in 1617, the trading post finally began to develop into a real settlement. Though several more disasters struck, it was never completely abandoned.

New France under Company Rule

The French king wanted a colony in Canada which would eventually bring added glory and wealth to France. The colony, therefore, had to be strong enough to resist attack by either European or Indian enemies. But the king was unwilling to pay for all this. To solve his problem, he turned to the increasingly profitable fur trade.

He granted a charter to a small group of merchants and gave them sole control of the fur trade in New France and sole right to sell the furs in the mother country. In return for these privileges, the merchants agreed to bring out settlers and support the young colony by paying for its government. This system of monopolies lasted until 1663. Although it had some obvious advantages, it also had many disadvantages, the main one being uncertainty. If the king granted a monopoly, he could just as easily cancel it. Because of the profits to be made, there were always many competitors seeking the king's favor. The monopoly did, in fact, change hands several times, with the result that trade was frequently disrupted. Moreover, the traders never quite knew where they stood and were unwilling to plan for the future.

In 1627, therefore, the French government awarded the monopoly to a new company, the Company of New France. This was a large, well-financed company which included many famous Frenchmen on its board of directors in Paris. It had a hundred shareholders and was popularly known as the Company of One Hundred Associates. In return for a fifteen-year trade monopoly and control of all French lands in North America, the company agreed to do three things: to govern and defend New France, to bring out settlers so that within fifteen years the population would number 4000, and to strengthen the Roman Catholic church by bringing out priests and missionaries.

The company's ambitious plans soon ran into difficulties. In 1628 an English force captured the ships bringing settlers and provisions; in the following year it seized Quebec, which remained in English hands until 1632. Threatened by financial problems and the hostility of the Iroquois, the company kept going only by leasing its fur-trade monopoly to other companies while continuing to rule the colony. The company also sold seigniories to landlords who agreed to bring out more colonists. Despite these efforts and those of the church, however, the population of New France grew very slowly and numbered only 2500 by 1663.

The Colony Expands

All the same, many changes had occurred in New France and in the fur trade since the foundation of Quebec in 1608. The most obvious change was the expansion of the colony.

Quebec grew steadily, if slowly, and soon replaced Tadoussac as the fur centre of New France. But as the demand for furs continued to increase, Champlain and his successors had to make sure of a regular supply. Champlain was both colonizer and explorer. He was fascinated by the stories he heard of the vast interior regions and impressed by the birchbark canoes, which he knew would help him penetrate into the unknown wilderness.

Indian Alliances

Any extension of trade, of course, meant getting involved in the fierce tribal hostilities of the Indians. At first the Montagnais and Algonquins, who lived on the northern shore of the St. Lawrence, provided furs and acted as middlemen for the tribes in the interior. But as the other tribes became aware of the goods and weapons traded by the French, more of them wanted to join in. One Indian, who clearly saw the value of the trade, commented with considerable understanding: "In truth, my brothers, the beaver does everything to perfection. He makes for us better kettles, axes, swords, knives, and gives us drink and food without the trouble of cultivating the ground." As could only be expected, competition for the trade aggravated the hostility that had long existed between the Iroquois and their neighbors, the Hurons, Montagnais and Algonquins.

From the start Champlain aided the Algonquins and Montagnais against the Iroquois. As early as 1609, he explored the Richelieu River as far as Lake Champlain and helped to defeat an Iroquois war party. That victory was easy, but once the Iroquois obtained modern weapons from the Dutch, who had colonies just

Like many missionaries and coureurs de bois, Father François-Joseph le Mercier, who lived among the Hurons and Iroquois for twenty years, adopted many of the Indians' ways in order to survive.

to the south, they became and long remained a real danger to the French and their Indian allies.

Knowing that the fur trade depended on regular supplies coming down the Ottawa River from the Huron country, Champlain sent many a young man from Quebec to live among the Indians there. They would learn the Indians' languages and customs, and try to win their friendship. The most famous of these young adventurers was Etienne Brûlé, who spent several winters with different tribes and who may well have travelled as far west as Lake Superior.

In 1613 Champlain made a trip up the Ottawa River and then, two years later, undertook his greatest exploration. To aid the Hurons against the Iroquois, he travelled up the Ottawa River, across the Mattawa to Lake Nipissing and down the French River to Georgian Bay. From there he made his way down to the land south of Lake Ontario. Although his attack on the Iroquois failed, his journey encouraged many others to follow his example.

New Settlements—Trois-Rivières and Montreal

In the following years, French traders pushed farther inland up the rivers. They would often take their trade goods, live with the Indians during the winter and then return to the trading posts in the spring with their cargo of furs. As these trading trips gradually opened up the lands to the west of the St. Lawrence, the settlement of New France itself also expanded.

In 1634 Trois-Rivières began as a small trading post on the northern shore of the St. Lawrence, 125 kilometres upstream from Quebec. Then, eight years later, Montreal was founded as a mission on an island located where the Ottawa River flows into the St. Lawrence. In the spring, these posts—and particularly Montreal—were the scene of the annual fur fairs. These were lively and picturesque events. The Indians would come down to trade their furs in the time-honored fashion, and the coureurs de bois added to the excitement. After a season spent in the woods, these adventurous traders were determined to give full vent to their high spirits. Their celebrations all too often ended in bouts of drunkenness which earned them a reputation as a rather wild lot.

Montreal began as a mission post called Ville-Marie and serves as a useful reminder of the important part that missionaries played in the life of New France. Missionaries had come out to Port Royal to win converts among the neighboring Indian tribes even before Champlain established Quebec. The first missionaries in Quebec were three Recollet fathers who arrived in 1615. When they realized how great their task was, they sought help from the Jesuits, who arrived in 1625 and almost immediately set out to work among the Hurons. As they penetrated deeper into Huron territory, the Jesuit missionaries learned much about the geography of the region. This knowledge was very valuable to the many explorers who later crossed this area. But the Jesuits also suffered many hardships as they tried to win the respect and friendship of the Hurons. Their work was far from easy. Many Indians understandably resented missionaries who tried to make them give up their religion and accept a new God. "Christianity," said one Huron, "is good for the French; we are another people with different customs."

The Jesuits persevered, however, and finally established a mission called Sainte-Marie near Georgian Bay. Protected by walls, it included a hospital, chapel, lodgings and a farm with crops and livestock. From this centre, they set up smaller missions throughout the Huron lands. But their efforts soon received a severe setback. In the 1640s the Iroquois, now better armed with modern weapons, renewed their attacks. They desperately needed furs to trade for European weapons and utensils, and they could get them only by subduing their neighbors. If they could destroy New France and its Indian allies, they would be able to trade freely and profitably with the Dutch on the Hudson River.

The Fight for Survival

The French could not defend the many kilometres of waterways linking their small settlements at Quebec, Trois-Rivières and Montreal with the fur-rich lands to the north and west. The first of many attacks took place in 1642 when the Iroquois ambushed Huron canoes bringing furs down to Quebec. As the attacks continued, the Indian allies of the French naturally became frightened and hesitated to bring in their furs. Trade dwindled to a trickle. Then, in 1648, the Iroquois turned their full fury against the Hurons and their French allies. The missions were abandoned, many priests were killed and the Hurons ceased to exist as a nation.

By this time, of course, the fur trade was almost at a standstill. One Jesuit reported in 1653:

> Before the devastation of the Hurons, a hundred canoes used to come to trade, all laden with Beaver-skins; and each year we had two or three hundred thousand livres' worth. That was a fine revenue with which to satisfy all the people, and defray the heavy expenses of the country . . .
>
> The Iroquois war dried up all these springs. The Beavers are left in peace and in the place of their repose; the Huron fleets no longer come down to trade; the Algonquins are depopulated; and the more distant Nations are withdrawing still farther, fearing the fire of the Iroquois.

New France was fighting for its life. Bands of Iroquois constantly threatened the settlements. In the spring of 1660, a gallant stand by Dollard des Ormeaux and his sixteen companions at the Long

Sault Rapids on the Ottawa River may have saved Montreal from destruction. The young Frenchmen all lost their lives, but the encounter dissuaded the Iroquois from further attack. New France was safe, but hardly flourishing.

The colony had suffered many hardships. The population was still small, and the missionaries had only had partial success. The fur trade, on which the colony depended for its wealth and even for its very existence, had virtually been destroyed. A drastic change was needed if the colony were ever to prosper. This change came in 1663 with the imposition of royal government, and it came just in time.

Royal government was strong government. French regular soldiers defeated the Iroquois and regained control of the Ottawa River trade route. Immigration and new industries strengthened the colony and restored the morale of the people. But then came a new threat. In 1664 the English captured the Dutch colonies to the south and now controlled much of the Atlantic coast and the Hudson River route to the interior. Just seven years later, through the adventurous exploits of two young Frenchmen, Pierre Esprit Radisson and Médard Chouart, later Sieur des Groseilliers, the English also established themselves on Hudson Bay. The fur trade of New France would be threatened from two sides.

Rivals for the Trade

Chapter **3**

In the 1650s the Iroquois threats had almost brought the fur trade to a standstill. But while many traders were much too timid to face the possibility of an Iroquois attack, there were always a few brave and adventuresome young men who would willingly risk their lives to make a quick profit in furs. Radisson and Groseilliers were two such men.

The Adventures of Radisson and Groseilliers

Groseilliers, whose name means "gooseberry," was born in France in 1618. He came to Quebec about 1641 and first learned something about the western lands by working with the Jesuits among the Hurons. Later, he and an unknown companion spent two full years trying to reopen the fur trade routes which the Iroquois had closed. According to the Jesuits, who kept a written record of most things that happened in New France, "universal joy" greeted their eventual return with fifty canoes laden with furs. After several years of almost no trade, no wonder the people were excited! Perhaps the colony could survive after all.

Groseilliers was also able to tell the colonists more about the lands to the west. He told them that "there are in the Northern region many Lakes which might be called freshwater Seas, the great Lake of the Hurons, and another near it, being as large as the Caspian Sea." He had also heard of "many Nations surrounding the Nation of the Sea which some have called 'the Stinkards,' because its people formerly lived on the shores of the Sea, which they call Ouinipeg, that is, 'stinking water.' " On this journey

29

Groseilliers stayed for a time at Green Bay on Lake Michigan, and it is possible that others in his party may even have reached the Mississippi.

In 1659 the restless Groseilliers again set out from his home in Trois-Rivières for the West. This time he took along his young brother-in-law, Pierre Esprit Radisson. They were almost ready to leave when the governor insisted they take one of his servants with them. But the two adventurers were determined to be free to make their own plans. So they said nothing then slipped out quietly to meet their Indian guides at a prearranged place on the St. Lawrence River.

It was an exciting and eventful journey. To begin with, they only just avoided an Iroquois attack on the Ottawa River. Then it took all their skill and strength to negotiate the treacherous waters near Lake Nipissing. With great relief they finally reached the calm waters of Lake Huron, where paddling was easier and where there was little danger from the Iroquois. They then made their way through the narrow waters into Lake Superior and spent some time at Chequamegon Bay on its southern shore. There they built a little fort and feasted the Indians they met with the wild animals and fowl which they shot. While making friends, they missed no opportunity to trade for furs. They also thoroughly enjoyed the attention and respect they received from the Indians who had never seen Europeans before. Young Radisson, who was a keen storyteller and a bit of an actor, must particularly have enjoyed this new and strange audience even if they did not always understand some of his wild and fanciful tales.

But soon it was time for the two Frenchmen and their Indian guides to move on. As winter set in, they faced the threat of starvation. Heavy snowfalls made it impossible to kill game, and it was only with the goodwill of the Indians they met that they were able to survive. In the spring, laden with furs, they set out from Lake Superior to return home. Passing by the site of Dollard's stand at the Long Sault, they saw the bodies of the French heroes. They reached Montreal late in August and then continued on to Trois-Rivières and Quebec.

Their return to New France with a rich cargo of furs again

probably saved the colony. According to Mother Marie de l'Incarnation, head of the Ursuline convent in Quebec, the fur merchants had been just about to leave the country, "believing that nothing further could be done for its trade."

It was the custom for the Company of New France to take as a tax one-quarter of the value of all furs brought into the colony. The cargo of furs collected by Groseilliers and Radisson was so large that the tax on it accounted for most of the colony's income. Everyone should have been very pleased, but unfortunately, the governor was still furious because the two adventurers had left without his permission. He imposed a heavy fine on them and even imprisoned Groseilliers for a short time. This seemed a harsh punishment, but it was not entirely undeserved. Illegal trading, the governor thought, weakened the colony by attracting the youngest and most adventuresome men. Many of them were bored with a dull life on the farm and eagerly seized the chance for the thrill and danger of trading with the Indians. But if they were out in the forests, who would be left to till the soil and protect the colonists? If only a few men went, there might be no danger; but as more and more left, the governor tried to put a stop to it. He was only partly successful, for by 1680 there were as many as eight hundred illegal traders.

Groseilliers and Radisson were, of course, disgusted at the actions of the governor, and they decided to turn their backs on an ungrateful New France. During their last journey west they had learned that the finest furs came from the land of the Cree beyond Lake Superior. They had also learned that the best way to bring out the furs would probably be by the much shorter route to the shores of Hudson Bay. In the next few years they made plans to reach the Bay, but their attempts to do so were unsuccessful. They did turn up in New England, however. It was from there that the English government heard of their exploits and their reports of furs in the North. In 1665 they accepted an invitation to England and took with them furs valued at £500 when they sailed.

They obviously knew how to impress King Charles and his courtiers. Radisson always liked to put on a show, and he was determined to win English support for their planned venture to

32

In 1668 Groseilliers set sail from England on the ketch Nonsuch *and reached the shores of James Bay. His success led to the formation of the Hudson's Bay Company. The* Nonsuch, *built in 1650, was probably manned by a crew of eight or ten. An exact replica, shown here sailing off Toronto, is now on display at the Manitoba Museum of Man and Nature in Winnipeg.*

Hudson Bay. He went into the king's presence dressed as an Indian chief and then held the court spellbound by his exciting and wildly exaggerated tales. He falsely claimed to have reached the shores of Hudson Bay and asserted that it took only seven days by canoe from the Bay to Lake Winnipeg, and from there only another seven days to the "South Sea," or Pacific Ocean.

King Charles probably did not believe all these claims, but he was amused and interested enough to promise his support. After three years of preparations, Groseilliers and Radisson set sail for Hudson Bay, Groseilliers in the *Nonsuch* and Radisson in the *Eaglet*. Unfortunately the two ships encountered heavy storms in the North Atlantic. The *Eaglet* lost its mast in a gale and turned back to England, but the *Nonsuch* persevered on through Hudson Strait and down to the mouth of the Rupert River which flows into James Bay. By this time it was already September, and Groseilliers prepared to spend the winter on this rocky shoreline. He immediately put his men to work, and very soon they had built a small palisaded fort which they named Fort Charles in honor of the king. Though they may not have fully realized it, they were on the fringes of the richest beaver country of North America.

Next spring over three hundred Indians came to trade furs, and the *Nonsuch* returned to England with a rich cargo. This success quickly won the support of the English government and of a group of eighteen wealthy men. In the following year these men received from the king a royal charter as "The Governor and Company of Adventurers of England Trading into Hudson's Bay." The first Governor was Prince Rupert, who was the cousin of King Charles.

The Hudson's Bay Company

The new company received enormous powers. Its main interest, of course, was in the valuable fur trade, and the charter granted it "the sole Trade and Commerce of all those Seas Streightes Bayes Rivers Lakes Creekes and Soundes in whatever Latitude they shall bee that lie within the entrance of the Streightes commonly called Hudsons Streightes." The members of the company, however, were to be more than traders; they were also to be "the true and absolute Lordes and Proprietors'' of the vast area which drained into Hudson Bay.

In return for this grant of almost half a continent, the company promised to pay to the king ''two Elkes and two Black beavers whensoever and as often as Wee our heires and successors shall happen to enter into the said Countryes Territoryes and Regions hereby granted.'' This was a very good bargain for the company— it paid no rent for over two hundred years!

As soon as the charter had been granted, the new company sent two ships to the Bay. The crews spent the winter in the cramped and dismal Fort Charles, and in the spring they carried on a brisk trade with the Indians. They took back a full cargo of furs, which were put up for sale in the first public fur auction in London at Garraway's Inn in January, 1672.

Realizing the riches that awaited on the Bay, the company lost no time in sending out three ships that summer. But this time an unpleasant surprise awaited them. Nailed to the walls of Fort Charles they found the royal arms of France! Two daring Frenchmen had reached the fort overland from Quebec and had left the plaque to show the English that in the future they could expect some competition.

This certainly spurred the English on to strengthen their position on the Bay. Within two years they built Fort Albany and Moose Factory. To these they later added York Factory in 1682 and the short-lived Fort Severn in 1685.

French-English Rivalry over Hudson Bay

The French quickly responded to all this activity by renewing their efforts to penetrate into the rich fur regions of the interior. At first they turned west and built trading posts on the northern shores of the Great Lakes. Later, they turned south along the Mississippi and gradually won control of the lands all the way to the Gulf of Mexico.

Of course, the French posts along the Mississippi posed no threat to the Hudson's Bay Company. But once the French had begun to probe to the North, there was bound to be trouble sooner or later. Both the English and the French naturally tried to persuade

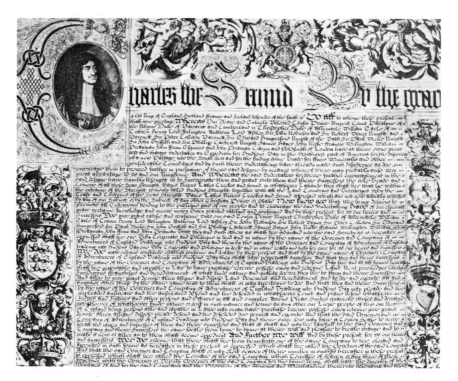

First page of the Hudson's Bay Company Charter granted by King Charles II of England in 1670.

the Indians to bring their furs to them; and they missed few chances to attack their rivals' forts. In these skirmishes, the French often seemed to have the advantage. They were daring in their attacks and they knew better than the English how to travel and survive in the vast forests that reached almost to the shores of the Bay.

The English traders, on the other hand, showed little imagination. Just occasionally an Englishman would make a daring trip to the interior. One such man was Henry Kelsey, who in 1690-1692 got as far as The Pas in present-day Manitoba. Most of the traders, though, made no attempt to explore the interior of the country and were content to sit in their posts waiting each spring for the Indians to bring down their furs. They would then barter their trade goods—muskets, powder, tools and utensils—for furs which they sent home to England for auction. It was a dreary life, especially during the long and bitterly cold winter, and sometimes they would get careless. This was when the French would strike. The English soon began to realize that their long distance from New France was no guarantee of safety from a daring enemy.

In 1686, for example, the French sent more than a hundred men in thirty-five canoes to attack the English posts on James Bay. They took the English traders at Moose Factory completely by surprise in the middle of the night. The English, still clad only in their nightshirts, put up a feeble resistance and soon surrendered. Similar attacks occurred almost every year, and trading posts regularly changed hands. Then, in 1697, the fighting moved dramatically to the sea and became much more serious.

The first public auction of Hudson's Bay Company furs was held in 1672 in the hall of Garraway's Inn, a famous London coffee house where the wits, beaux and well-to-do merchants of the period gathered. Both the Prince of Wales and the Duke of York were among the spectators, as were many other distinguished men. A lighted candle on the auctioneer's desk was the most common method of limiting bids at fur auctions: when the flame went out, bidding ceased.

Under orders from Governor Frontenac of New France, the renowned Le Moyne d'Iberville led a fleet of five ships in a determined attempt to clear the English from the Bay once and for all. The French ships entered Hudson Strait only a day and a half after four ships from England. When separated from his other ships, d'Iberville spotted the English fleet and closed for action. Though badly outnumbered and outgunned, he took on the English ships single-handed and a bitter battle raged for four hours. English guns and muskets raked the French ship, but d'Iberville repelled all attempts to board. Then suddenly the tide of battle turned. The largest English warship sank with the loss of 290 crew members. A second ship surrendered, and a third escaped to the mouth of the Nelson River. D'Iberville, determined to press home his advantage, then laid seige to York Factory with a force of 900 men. After holding out for four days, the English garrison surrendered and marched out of the fort with the honors of war—arms, drum and flag.

The French now held the best trading centre on Hudson Bay while the English could only operate from Fort Albany on James Bay. But the English still had one advantage. Their stronger navy could prevent French ships from getting to and from York Factory. Neither side was really winning, and the fur trade was declining rapidly. In 1713, however, England and France made peace after a long series of wars in Europe by signing the Treaty of Utrecht. Under the terms of the treaty, the French finally recognized the English claim to Hudson Bay. The Hudson's Bay Company now regained its lost trading posts and could look forward to a future free from direct French attack.

The removal of the French threat helped the Hudson's Bay Company traders, but it also kept them lazy and contented. They still showed little interest in exploration or in building inland forts. The French, on the other hand, were planning for the future. They had not really minded giving up their posts on the Bay because they knew they would find it difficult to keep them supplied. The overland route was far too long, and their navy was no match for that of the English who could control all shipping into Hudson Bay. But they were not prepared to sit back and let the English

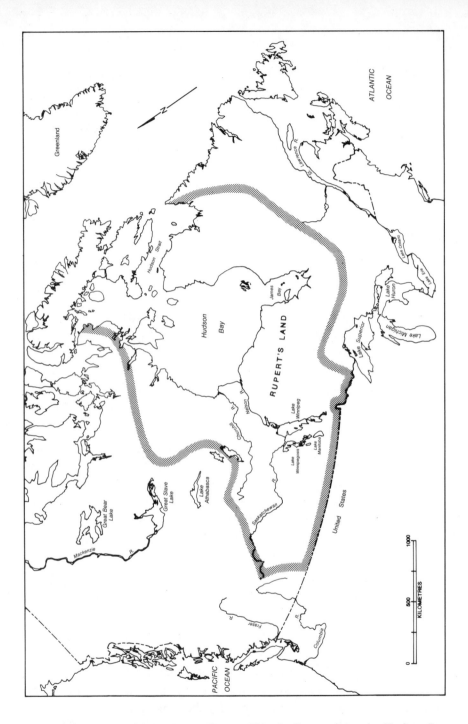

Map showing Canada's main waterways. The shading outlines the Hudson Bay drainage basin, that is, the territory granted to the Hudson's Bay Company.

have it all their own way. If the French could not compete on the Bay, they would try other means to divert furs from the English. This they could do by building inland posts much closer to the Indians who supplied the furs. The Indians could surely be persuaded to trade with a nearby French post rather than take their furs hundreds of kilometres to the English posts on the Bay.

The French Establish Themselves in the Northwest

While the leaders of New France, men like Intendant Jean Talon and Governor Frontenac, were building up the colony and making it more secure, hundreds of traders, missionaries, soldiers and Indians were exploring the vast unknown lands to the north, west and south. At the same time that Groseilliers and Radisson were paving the way for the English to the north, Talon decided on a bold plan of expansion aimed at preventing the English colonists on the Atlantic seaboard from moving westward across the Allegheny Mountains. As early as 1670, Talon decided to claim for France all the lands to the west which were still unclaimed. He sent an officer, Daumont de Saint-Lusson, to Sault Ste. Marie, which was an important crossroads of the three Upper Great Lakes. There, in a dramatic and colorful ceremony, Saint-Lusson planted a huge cross with the royal arms of France, raised his sword and a sod of earth, and proclaimed French dominion to the assembled and probably baffled Indians.

In this exciting period of the history of New France, the work of the fur trader, the missionary and the explorer were all very closely connected. Sometimes the missionary saw the opportunity for trading; sometimes the fur trader became an explorer; sometimes the explorer became a fur trader. In an incredible burst of energy, New France explored and claimed half a continent.

Louis Jolliet and the Jesuit priest, Jacques Marquette, discovered the Mississippi River in 1672 and descended it as far as the Arkansas River. Then, ten years later, La Salle completed the work by reaching the delta where the city of New Orleans stands today. He dreamed of a great fur-trading empire stretching from the Gulf of St. Lawrence to the Gulf of Mexico. Within twenty years of his death in 1684, his dreams seemed to be coming true.

HALFMOON BAY ELEMENTARY

Although the exploration of the Mississippi led to French domination of the vast area later known as Louisiana, the region was not good fur country. The exploration of the Canadian prairies was far more important for the fur trade. The key to this exploration, and possibly the key to a route to the long-sought western sea, was Lake Winnipeg. This lake was the junction of the routes to the west and the routes coming from the East. The French had long known of this lake through Indian tradition. If they could discover its exact location, they would have a strong base for further exploration and for a vast extension of the fur trade.

Just a few years after Kelsey journeyed south from Hudson Bay to the prairies, a great French explorer penetrated to the same area by the route from Lake Superior. His name was Pierre Gaultier de Varennes, Sieur de La Vérendrye.

La Vérendrye and his Sons Explore the West

La Vérendrye grew up on his grandfather's seigniory near Montreal in the days when the danger of Indian attack was never far distant. From men like La Salle, the famous explorer of the Mississippi, and other visitors to the seigniory, young Pierre heard exciting tales which stirred his restless and adventuresome spirit. At the age of twelve he joined the local militia unit as a cadet, and by the time he was twenty he was serving with the colonial troops. In 1707, he sailed to France and enlisted in the regular army. He took part in several battles, was wounded and taken prisoner.

Perhaps by this time, war had lost some of its appeal, for in 1711 he suddenly returned to New France. He settled at Trois-Rivières and spent the next fifteen years trading for furs, raising a family of four sons and two daughters, and learning all he could from the Indians who brought him their furs.

The unknown western lands fascinated him, and in 1727 La Vérendrye joined his brother at Fort Ste. Anne on Lake Nipigon. In the following year he became commander of the northern post at Kaministikwia, and it was there that his plans gradually took shape. He was excited by Indian reports of a great western lake from which a river flowed farther west into yet another great lake. Did this point the way to the western sea?

Shortly after La Vérendrye and his sons established their forts in the Northwest, the Hudson's Bay Company began sending out expeditions from its forts on the Bay to contact the Indians and persuade them to bring down their furs to trade. In 1754 Anthony Henday left York Factory and reached the foothills of the Rockies. The first white man to meet the Blackfoot Indians, he is shown here entering their camp near the present city of Red Deer, Alberta.

La Vérendrye sought the support of the governor in Quebec. Impressed by a rough sketch map showing possible routes to the West, the governor gave his enthusiastic approval of an expedition, as did the French government. But while they favored the proposed expedition, they refused to pay for it. Instead, they granted La Vérendrye a monopoly of the fur trade in the Northwest. This meant that he would have to borrow money against his expected profits. Once again the fur trade was to pay for government plans.

This was disappointing to La Vérendrye, for it meant that he would not be able to press onward as fast as he would have liked. The people who lent him money wanted to be sure that they made a profit or at least got their money back. La Vérendrye would have to stop and build forts to maintain and strengthen the fur trade.

At last his preparations were complete. Accompanied by three of his sons, Jean-Baptiste, Pierre and François, and by his nephew, Christophe de La Jemerais, he left Montreal in June, 1731, and made his way rapidly to the mouth of the Pigeon River, south of Kaministikwia. There, he spent the winter gathering furs.

Over the next three years, La Vérendrye and his party busily explored routes to the West and established forts at strategic points—Fort St. Pierre on Rainy Lake, Fort St. Charles on Lake of the Woods and Fort Maurepas on the shores of Lake Winnipeg. Whenever he stopped, he always reminded the Indians that it was essential for them to bring him furs of all kinds and in good supply. After all, he warned them, they needed his trade goods and it cost a lot to bring these all the way from Montreal.

After a quick visit to Quebec in 1734, La Vérendrye returned to the West the following year, only to meet growing misfortunes. His nephew took ill and died, then his son Jean-Baptiste was killed by a band of Sioux at Lake of the Woods. Although greatly upset, La Vérendrye continued his work undaunted. He set out with two of his sons in 1738 to penetrate farther west. Pushing quickly ahead, they built Fort La Reine on the Assiniboine River and Fort Rouge on the site of the modern city of Winnipeg. From Fort Rouge they turned south to the land of the Mandans on the banks of the Missouri. There, they were lured on by stories of white people living farther downriver. When told, however, that it would take an entire summer to reach these people, La Vérendrye reluctantly decided to return home. Convinced that the Missouri flowed southwest, he felt sure that he had found the route to the elusive western sea. He decided to continue his exploration later.

Fort La Reine became the party's base in 1741. From there his son Pierre travelled north and built Fort Dauphin on Lake Manitoba and Fort Bourbon on the northern part of Lake Winnipeg. Two other sons, Louis-Joseph and François, pushed farther west and may well have seen the foothills of the Rockies before returning to Fort Maurepas in 1743. In that year, burdened with debts, La Vérendrye returned home to face his creditors. Only later did he

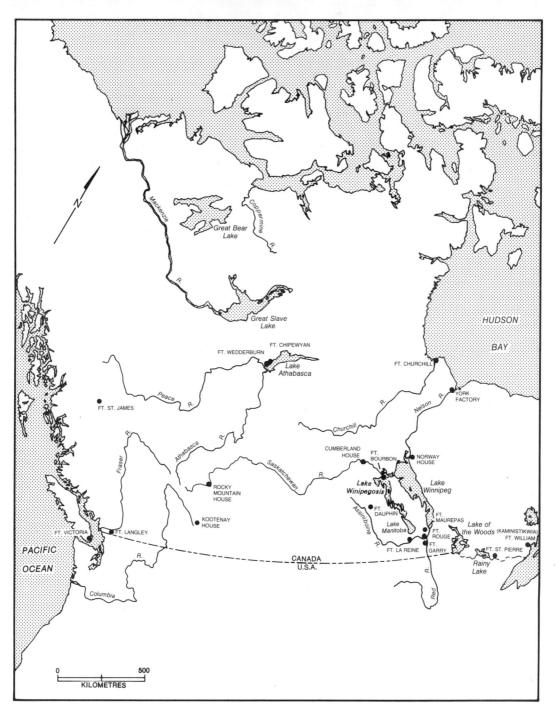

Map of western Canada with the most important trading posts established by the La Vérendryes and the North West and Hudson's Bay companies.

begin to receive the fame due to him for his incredible exploits.

The La Vérendryes were a remarkable family and their achievements were equally remarkable. With unbounded courage and indomitable spirit, they pushed farther west than any previous explorer. With only half-hearted support from the government and in face of the jealous plots of the fur traders in New France, they opened up a vast area to French influence and French trade. Their string of forts reached all the way to the Saskatchewan River and were so well placed that the Indians could easily bring their furs there and save themselves the long and often dangerous journey to the English posts on Hudson Bay.

Later, other French traders improved the portages and trails and organized an efficient system of supplying food and goods to these outlying forts by building a large trading centre at Kaministikwia to store goods brought out from Montreal during the short summer season.

Thus, in the continuing competition for furs, the French, largely through the efforts of La Vérendrye and his sons, had greatly strengthened their position against the English. Trade improved, and the sale of furs in France increased.

But just as New France was about to reap the benefits of its expanded trade, the colony suddenly faced its most serious threat. War broke out in North America between Britain and France, and the French faced superior military and naval forces. On September 13, 1759, Wolfe defeated Montcalm at the Battle of the Plains of Abraham. New France was soon to pass under British rule.

Two Great Companies

Chapter **4**

New France became a British colony in 1763. This removed the French threat to the Hudson's Bay Company. But the Montreal merchants who had previously invested in the fur trade were still eager for business, and the long string of fur-trading posts reaching far out to the West were still standing. What would happen now to this vast fur-trading organization with its employees, its forts, its trails and portages and its supply system?

Experienced traders soon saw their chance. Many came north from the New England colonies to join those already in Montreal. They realized that they could not work very effectively by themselves, so they soon formed partnerships. Some of these partnerships were quite small and consisted of just a few traders who divided up the work: one might get the furs, another would sell them, and a third would look after supplies.

These adventurous traders quickly fell under the spell of the great northwest, a largely unknown land of possible danger but also of great profit. The more daring soon reached the area around Lake Winnipeg, and when they returned to Montreal with rich loads of furs, the rush to the West really began. Adventure and profit spurred them on, and nothing was going to stop them as they reoccupied the forts built by the La Vérendryes and pushed even farther north and west.

Sometimes they would meet men of the Hudson's Bay Company who reminded them that they were trespassing on lands belonging to their company by the charter of 1670. This did not worry the new traders. They felt that they not only had a right to

This half-size birchbark canoe could carry two tonnes of supplies in addition to the crew. The packages, or pièces, *each weighed forty-two kilograms. Notice the use of the tumpline, or forehead band, to steady and support the pièces.*

the abandoned French posts, but also a right to trade wherever they wanted. They would not obey laws which could not be enforced.

This flurry of activity had one drawback. Because the new traders were often working in very small groups, there was keen competition between them. This, of course, helped the Indians, who could haggle over the value of the furs they were selling and hold out for top prices. The traders soon realized that they would do better if they joined forces. In that way they would pay less for the furs and the Indians would pay more for their trade goods. The only alternative the Indians had was to go all the way to the Hudson's Bay Company posts on the Bay.

The North West Company

After a time, a number of these trading groups formed the North West Company. This company was very different from the Hudson's Bay Company. It had no charter from the king; it had no large number of shareholders in Britain. It was really more like a series of partnerships which joined together to help each other. Some of the partners naturally had more influence than others, and they were the ones who usually decided what should be done.

The new company started in 1783, the year in which the American colonists became independent from Britain and therefore could no longer take part in the fur trade in Canada. But although the company had no great fear of American rivals, it did have several competitors within Canada. The most important of these was the New North West Company, founded at Montreal in 1798 and popularly known as the XY Company. It took this name in order to avoid confusion with the North West Company, which used the letters NW to label its goods. The new company simply adopted the next two letters after W and marked its goods XY. For several years there was bitter hostility, which ended only when the two companies merged in 1804. When that happened, the North West Company reorganized on the basis of 100 shares, of which the former XY Company received 25.

Perhaps because so many of the North West traders were used to keen competition from their rivals, they were imaginative, hard working and often ruthless. They were working for themselves, not to make profits for shareholders in Britain, and they threw themselves wholeheartedly into their business.

The officers and men of the Hudson's Bay Company, still sitting in their posts on Hudson Bay, often laughed at the Nor'Westers, as the North West Company traders were called. They sneeringly termed them ''pedlars'' because they did so much of the carrying of goods and furs, while the Hudson's Bay men simply waited for the Indians to bring in their furs and carry away their trade goods.

Although the Hudson's Bay men might sneer at the Nor'Westers, they had had to begin changing their ways. The inland forts of their trade rivals were attracting many Indians who

Samuel Hearne builds Cumberland House, 1774-75. This was the first inland trading post built by the Hudson's Bay Company and was situated in modern Saskatchewan. Here Hearne discusses the building plans with the carpenter. Note the log tent in which Hearne and his men spent the winter.

might otherwise have gone to the Bay. After sitting for a hundred years on the shores of the Bay, the company men had finally realized they would have to move inland if they were to beat back the competition. They had taken the first step in 1774. Samuel Hearne had just returned from his epic journey to the shores of the Arctic Ocean, and the company sent him to build its first inland trading post, Cumberland House, on the Saskatchewan River.

The competition between the Hudson's Bay and North West companies gradually grew bitter. The Nor'Westers built up a very efficient organization in order to challenge the well-established older company. But they had a much bigger problem in getting supplies to their traders and taking the furs back to headquarters. The Hudson's Bay Company enjoyed the comparatively short supply route of only 700 kilometres between York Factory, where the ocean-going supply ship arrived each summer, and Norway House at the northern end of Lake Winnipeg. From Norway House, two main routes ran 500 kilometres to Cumberland House and 600 kilometres to Fort Rouge at the junction of the Red and Assiniboine rivers. Both these routes were relatively short and simple, although at times they could be dangerous.

The North West Company, on the other hand, faced a more difficult situation. The Athabasca region, which was extremely rich in furs and which was just being opened up, was 6000 kilometres from the company headquarters in Montreal. Not only that, but there were only five months between spring break-up and winter freeze-up, and the large freight canoes could average only 2000 kilometres a month. Adding to the problem was the fact that the large canoes suitable for the main rivers and the Great Lakes were far too big for the smaller rivers and for the portages to the west of Lake Superior. The company tackled these difficulties with imagination.

The headquarters of the North West Company remained in Montreal. Every spring, brigades of canoes left nearby Lachine bound for the West and fully laden with trade goods, food and supplies. Their immediate destination was Fort William, which became the western headquarters of the company in 1804. Here, each summer, the Montreal partners arrived to meet and discuss company business with the "wintering partners," who spent the winter in the West. Fort William stood on the site of Fort Kaministikwia on the western shore of Lake Superior. An impressive trading centre covering many hectares, it became the supply centre or *entrepot* for all the western fur trade. Each summer, Fort William's thriving little community burst into feverish activity when the brigades of *canots de maître* arrived carrying essential supplies and trade goods from Montreal. The trade goods included a wide variety of items that the Indians wanted—muskets, shot, gunpowder, cloth, blankets, knives, needles, thread, kettles, tobacco

For many years Fort William was the North West Company's most important depot. Its buildings included a large house for the partner in charge, a council house, a doctor's residence, several buildings to accommodate workmen and traders from the interior, a forge and various other workshops, extensive stores for trading goods and furs, and even a jail (familiarly known as the pot au beurre, "pot of butter"). Outside the walls were a shipyard, where the company's vessels were built and repaired, and a farm, where grain and vegetables were grown and animals raised for domestic use. The reconstructed fort pictured here is about twenty kilometres from the original site at Thunder Bay.

and brandy. At the same time, the smaller canoes laden with furs arrived from the outlying fur posts. Both parties met at Fort William, where a month was allowed for the crews to rest and for the company servants to sort and repack the furs and supplies. An exception was made for the crews bringing furs from Athabasca. They could not possibly get all the way to Fort William and back before the rivers and lakes froze over. To supply these men, several Montreal canoes went as far as the forwarding post at Lac La Pluie (Rainy Lake) where they exchanged their goods for furs and then returned to Montreal.

Company officers knew by experience almost exactly what supplies and food were needed for each part of the long route west. From Fort William to Lac la Pluie, for example, the ration for each canoe of five men consisted of "two bags of corn 1½ bushel each and 15 lb of grease." For longer trips, of course, they needed many more supplies, and all of these had to be taken from the stores at Fort William.

The Voyageurs

The North West Company depended for its very existence on the many thousands of kilometres of waterways reaching far west from Montreal, first to Fort William and then to the Athabasca country. The hero of these waterways was the voyageur.

The voyageurs were the men who paddled the canoes or rowed the larger boats which carried men and supplies over the rivers and lakes far to the north and west. They were usually French-Canadian or Métis, and they led a colorful but hard life. An army officer who travelled from Lachine to St. Joseph in 1798 wrote:

> No men in the world are more severely worked than are these Canadian voyageurs. I have known them to work in a canoe twenty hours out of twenty-four, and go at that rate during a fortnight or three weeks without a day of rest . . . They smoke almost incessantly, and sing peculiar songs, which are the same their fathers and grandfathers and probably their great grandfathers sang before them . . . They rest from five to ten minutes every two hours, when they refill their pipes; it is more common for them to describe distances by so many pipes, than in any other way.

Many travellers wrote or told stories about voyageurs and commented on their bright woven sashes, or *ceintures fléchées*, and their rhythmic songs. But their daily routine, when on a trip, was extremely demanding and the trips often lasted as many as six or eight weeks. They were roused as early as two or three in the morning. Unless there were rapids just ahead, they started off without breakfast, which they did not get until about eight. The midday meal often consisted of nothing more than a piece of pemmican to chew as they continued to paddle. Then, usually between eight and ten in the evening, depending on the light, they made camp and ate their supper. Exhausted after the long day's paddling, the men would enjoy a quiet smoke and then try to get some sleep. They lay on the ground with their heads under the overturned canoe, sheltered from the rain by a tarpaulin. They were constantly tormented by insects, especially mosquitoes and black flies, but they got some relief by lighting smudges a few paces away. These were fires piled high with damp moss or green leaves so that they gave off a dense, acrid smoke.

Apart from the long days of paddling and the many discomforts, there were also many real dangers, particularly at rapids and at the more difficult portages. Then the voyageurs, carrying two *pièces* of 40 kilograms each or helping to carry an inverted 300-kilogram canot de maître, had to struggle over rocks and through bogs and icy water. Many a voyageur died from injuries or from drowning. When this happened, his comrades buried him on the side of the trail and erected a crude wooden cross over his grave.

To many travellers, the voyageurs were the heroes of the fur trade, but to others they were very human people with many faults. Daniel Harmon, who spent twenty years in the fur trade, got to know the voyageurs very well. He praised them for their willingness to "submit to great privation and hardship, not only without complaining, but even with cheerfulness and gaiety." He also, however, described them as fickle, thoughtless, improvident, deceitful and vain. Like all people, in other words, the voyageurs had their good and their bad points. But they were essential to the fur trade, and they did their job well. John Jacob Astor, the prominent American fur trader, knew all their faults but still said

PEMMICAN

Like the food given to modern astronauts, pemmican was concentrated, nutritious and easily preserved. Paul Kane, the famous painter who travelled through western Canada in the 1840s, left one of the best descriptions of how pemmican was made from buffalo meat:

> The thin slices of dried meat are pounded between two stones until the fibres separate; about 50 lbs. of this are put into a bag of buffalo skin, with about 40 lbs. of melted fat, and mixed together while hot, and sewed up, forming a hard and compact mass; hence its name in the Cree language, *pimmi* signifying meat, and *kon*, fat . . . One pound of this is considered equal to four pounds of ordinary meat, and the pemmican keeps for years perfectly good exposed to any weather.

In the more northern regions moose meat was often used instead of buffalo, and later in the Rockies and nearer the west coast, the meat of sheep was used. Although the traders and voyageurs got used to the taste of pemmican and probably liked it, most other travellers did not. The Earl of Southesk, who travelled into the Rocky Mountains in 1860, left this comment:

> Had 'berry-pemmican' at supper. That is to say, the ordinary buffalo pemmican, with Saskatoom berries sprinkled through it at the time of making,—which acts as currant jelly does with venison, correcting the greasiness of the fat by a slightly acid sweetness . . . Berry-pemmican is usually the best of its kind, but poor is the best. Take scrapings from the driest outside corner of a very stale piece of cold roast beef, add to it lumps of tallowy rancid fat, then garnish all with long human hairs (on which string pieces, like beads, upon a necklace), and short hairs of oxen, or dogs, or both,—and you have a fair imitation of common pemmican, though I should rather suppose it to be less nasty. Pemmican is most endurable when uncooked. My men used to fry it with grease, sometimes stirring-in flour, and making a flabby mess, called "rubaboo," which I found almost uneatable.

that he would prefer one Canadian voyageur to any three others!

The Beaver Club

The men of the North West Company were determined, vigorous, boisterous and often ruthless, and they showed something of this spirit in the meetings of the famous Beaver Club in Montreal. Founded in 1785, it at first had nineteen members who had all wintered in the Northwest. Later the club increased to fifty-five members who met regularly every two weeks throughout the winter. They developed an elaborate set of rules, and those who broke them had to pay their fines in bottles of wine. They all dutifully wore their large gold medals at the Club meetings where they sat down to several hours of wining and dining. The climax to the evening was the "Grand Voyage." All the members sat on the floor in a row, as if they were in a great canoe, and made paddling motions while singing rousing voyageur songs. It was a noisy and often a drunken evening. At one meeting in 1808, for example, thirty-one members and guests drank twenty-nine bottles of Madeira and nineteen bottles of port! But amid all their boisterous celebrations, they did not forget the people to whom they owed their success. They always drank five traditional toasts: to the mother of all the saints; the king; the fur trade in all its branches; voyageurs, wives and children; and absent friends.

The Great Explorers of the Northwest

The Nor'Westers were ambitious men. Not content with penetrating deep into the Northwest, they were determined to reach the shores of the Arctic Ocean and to cross the barriers of the Rockies to the Pacific coast. As always, fur trading and exploring went hand in hand, and the Nor'Westers gave Canada some of its greatest explorers.

Without any doubt the three greatest were Alexander Mackenzie, Simon Fraser and David Thompson. But another man, Peter Pond, prepared the way for them. Pond, born in Connecticut, came north and began trading in furs on the Saskatchewan River in 1775. Three years later he crossed the Methye Portage from the Churchill River to the Athabasca and penetrated into the incredibly rich fur region that lay to the north. He may even have gone as far north as Great Slave Lake. Not only did he explore this new area, but he also proved the importance of pemmican as a staple food. Fur traders in the south could always shoot wild game if they ran out of food, but this became more difficult the farther north they went. There were fewer animals and the voyageurs could certainly not count on them for food. They really needed some kind of food that they could easily take with them.

Alexander Mackenzie

Alexander Mackenzie joined the North West Company in 1787 and was soon put in charge of the Athabasca region, where he supervised the building of Fort Chipewyan. From there, in 1789, he set out on the first of his great explorations, reaching the Arctic Ocean by the river which now bears his name. He, however, called it the River of Disappointment, for he had been seeking a river that flowed west to the Pacific.

Mackenzie was a great leader of men and a determined explorer, however. After a brief visit to England in 1791 to buy better navigational instruments, he returned to the Northwest, and two years later he set off again to seek a passage through the mountains to the Pacific.

Entering the mighty Peace River, Mackenzie and his companions paddled upstream against a strong current and the bitter cold of October. At a point in the upper reaches of the river, they built a small fort and settled down for the winter.

By next April Mackenzie was busy trading for furs and building new canoes. Sending the fur-laden canoes back to Fort Chipewyan, he then resumed his journey with six of his most loyal and dependable voyageurs. Battling rapids, cascades and falls, and often portaging through great forests of spruce, birch and poplar, they finally reached the Continental Divide—the point in the Rocky Mountains which divides the rivers flowing east and the rivers flowing west. They were the first Europeans to cross the Divide north of the Spanish territories. A portage of over eight hundred paces brought them to a small lake from which the waters flowed to the Pacific. But their troubles were not yet over. Strong

On his second great voyage of exploration, Alexander Mackenzie became the first white man to reach the Pacific Ocean overland north of Mexico.

currents and rocks smashed the frail birchbark canoes, and they constantly had to stop and patch them before they could continue their journey. At last they reached the big river they sought, the Fraser. When they realized that it must enter the Pacific far to the south of where they had hoped, Mackenzie decided to make his final trek overland to the coast, using whatever smaller streams he could find. At last he reached the Dean River and finally Dean Channel, where he left the following inscription on a rock: "Alexander Mackenzie, from Canada, by land, the twenty-second of July, one thousand seven hundred and ninety-three."

Mackenzie had reached the Pacific Ocean. The route proved to be too difficult for trade, but he had nevertheless accomplished a monumental task. In two great journeys he had opened up a route to the Far North through some of the best fur-producing regions in the world, and he had led the way and inspired others to seek a practical route to the west coast. Both Simon Fraser and David Thompson followed his lead.

Fraser and Thompson

In 1805 and 1806 Fraser established the first trading posts ever placed within the present boundaries of British Columbia. These were Fort McLeod and the famous Fort St. James, which later became the capital of the fur-trading district of New Caledonia. Fraser thus extended the North West Company's activities to the territory west of the Rocky Mountains, but his greatest accomplishment was perhaps the exploration in 1808 of the river later named after him. The journey, filled with difficulties and danger, was an extraordinary feat. Nonetheless, its results were a disappointment both to Fraser, who had thought he was descending the Columbia, and to the North West Company, because the river was too treacherous to serve as a trade route.

David Thompson crossed the Rockies in 1807 and built the first trading post on the Columbia River at Kootenay House. Four years later he descended the mighty river to its mouth, where to his intense disappointment, he found that the Americans had already built a trading post, Fort Astoria. Thompson was the first white man to travel the full length of the Columbia River. A greater achievement, however, than his actual explorations was his careful surveying of all the land he travelled through. In all, he accurately mapped the main travel routes through more than four million square kilometres of territory, and his work formed the basis for all later maps of the West.

The Competition for Furs Intensifies

Fur traders from several nations had already established themselves on the Pacific coast. Russian traders in Alaska had found a ready market in China for their harvest of sea-otter. Captain Cook had explored much of the coast northward from Vancouver Island and traded for sea-otter with the Indians at Nootka. Other adventurers soon followed in the hope of making quick profits, and the competition intensified. In 1811, John Jacob Astor organized the Pacific Fur Company to obtain control of the flourishing fur trade with China, which was then the world's richest fur market. That same year the company established Fort Astoria at the mouth of the Columbia River. The Nor'Westers, however, proved to be the most determined and the most successful. In 1813 they bought Fort Astoria from the Americans and won unrivalled control of the coastal fur trade from the Columbia River to Alaska.

Nonetheless, the rival Hudson's Bay Company was far from idle. Its traders had been slow to react to the threat posed by the Nor'Westers because all important decisions were made in London by men who had no first-hand knowledge of the country. Finally, however, they became more aggressive.

For some years Cumberland House remained their only important inland post. Then, in an incredible burst of energy, they built nineteen more inland posts by 1802. Many of these were little more than huts or small warehouses which could be abandoned when they were no longer required. Others were more impressive and were built at key locations. Most, whether large or small, stood very close to forts of the North West Company.

As the Hudson's Bay Company extended its posts into the interior, competition became keener and the rival traders seldom missed a chance to cheat their opponents. But they rarely came to blows. Daniel Harmon, a Nor'Wester, described in his journal a visit he paid to Fort Alexandria on the Assiniboine River in 1805:

> Last evening Mr. Chaboillez (manager N.W. Company) invited the people of the other two forts to a dance; and we had a real North-West country ball. When three-fourths of the people had drunk so much as to be incapable of walking straight the other fourth thought it was time to put an end to the ball, or rather bawl. This morning we were invited to breakfast at the Hudson's Bay House with a Mr. McKay and in the evening to a dance. This, however, ended more decently than the one of the preceding evening.

This spirit of keen but not unfriendly rivalry lasted until 1811 when the London Committee of the Hudson's Bay Company made a decision which altered the whole future of the fur trade in western Canada.

In that year Thomas Douglas, earl of Selkirk, bought control of the Hudson's Bay Company. A kind man, Selkirk was concerned about the poor Scottish crofters who were being forced off their land to make way for more profitable sheep grazing. To help them, he had already established colonies in eastern Canada where they could be re-settled. Now he turned his attention to the rich agricultural lands at the junction of the Red and Assiniboine rivers in present-day Manitoba. He purchased from the Hudson's Bay Company a huge area of 300,000 square kilometres which was to be called Assiniboia. Within a year, the first group of settlers arrived by way of York Factory.

This was almost like a declaration of war against the Nor'Westers. Assiniboia lay across their main route to the West. This area was also the main source of buffalo pemmican, the staple food of the voyageurs. Seeing their future threatened, the Nor'Westers sought allies. They found them in the Métis, who feared that a farming settlement would destroy their semi-nomadic way of life. Troubles came to a head in 1816 when a combined force of Nor'Westers and Métis destroyed the main settlement and killed its governor. Only the arrival of Selkirk himself in the following year ensured the future of the colony.

The competition between the two companies became more and more violent. Both suffered, and eventually only one course of action seemed reasonable: the two companies agreed to unite. The long rivalry was over.

The New Hudson's Bay Company

Chapter **5**

The union of the two rival companies took place in 1821. Despite their competition, which had for several years been violent, they were ready for the union. Quarrels between the Montreal partners and the wintering partners had weakened the North West Company, and the Hudson's Bay Company was weary of the long and bitter struggle which disrupted business and lessened profits. In addition, the British government wanted an end to strife which set British subjects against each other and which was gradually ruining the lucrative fur trade.

The Hudson's Bay Company Reorganizes

The agreement of 1821 was worked out in London by representatives of both companies. They united under the name of the Hudson's Bay Company, and the headquarters remained in England, where final decisions would be made by the London Committee. But the new company differed from the old in one important way: now, as in the old North West Company, the actual traders would have a voice in its running and would share in the annual profits.

The company received a twenty-one-year monopoly of the trade in Rupert's Land, which it ruled, and also in the lands to the far Northwest. With these grants, the company virtually controlled all of modern Canada from Ontario to the Rocky Mountains, and it still had trading posts in northern Quebec and Labrador as well. Nor was this all. In 1818 the British and American governments agreed to open to people of both countries the land west of the Rocky Mountains between Russian Alaska and Mexican California. This vast area was called the Oregon Territory. Within it, the British government gave its trading rights to the new company.

The company naturally faced some difficult problems at first. Because it had taken over all the trading posts of both former companies, it now had far more posts than it really needed. By 1821 the Nor'Westers had ninety-seven posts and the Hudson's Bay Company seventy-six. Many of these would have to be closed. Where there were two posts within a few kilometres of each other (and many were even closer than that), it was common sense to keep the one that was in better repair and to abandon the other. But when a post was closed, it meant that the trader and other employees would be out of a job.

The hatred between the employees of the two companies also posed a difficult problem. When a Nor'Wester had just spent ten years of his life fighting the men of the Hudson's Bay Company, it was hard for him suddenly to forget all this and to work with his former rivals as colleagues. If the Nor'Westers were to work efficiently, they must feel at home in the new company and know exactly what their duties were.

Partly for this reason, the 1821 agreement ordered a reorganization of the company. In the West there were to be two large regional departments: the Southern Department, ruled from Moose Factory, and the larger and more important Northern Department, ruled from different centres—usually York Factory, Norway House or Fort Garry. Each department had a governor who was in charge of all the fur-trading districts within the department.

The company had two ranks of officers or "commissioned gentlemen" who, like the wintering partners of the old North West Company, shared in the profits and in the running of the company. At first there were twenty-five chief factors and twenty-eight chief traders. Thirty-two of these had been Nor'Westers. Each year the governor met with his council, which included the chief factors of the department, to decide on transfers, promotions, prices, methods of improving trade and any other problems that came up during the year. The chief factors had a lot of influence, and only

Nicholas Garry, a London director of the Hudson's Bay Company, came to Canada in 1821 to help unite the rival companies. He travelled widely and is shown here with Simon McGillivray (with glasses) of the North West Company, James Bird of the Hudson's Bay Company and a clerk at Slave Falls on the Winnipeg River. Upper and Lower Fort Garry on the Red River were named in his honor.

a very strong governor would be able to impose his will on them. George Simpson was such a man.

Sir George Simpson

George Simpson was born in the north of Scotland. Orphaned at an early age, he went to live with his aunt, who sent him to a nearby school where he learned to read, write, do simple arithmetic and keep accounts accurately. There were few opportunities in that part of Scotland, however, so at the age of fourteen young Simpson followed the example of many others who had left to seek work in the larger towns and cities. But he was luckier than many, for he was given a job by an uncle who ran a trading company in London. In 1820, just when he was tiring of the monotonous work and yearning for a more exciting life, luck again came to his rescue. Two of his uncle's partners were related to Lord Selkirk, through whose influence they could get him into the Hudson's Bay Company. Simpson jumped at the chance to leave England for a new and adventurous life in Rupert's Land.

Soon after Simpson arrived in Montreal, he learned that the Nor'Westers had seized the company's chief officer in the Athabasca district. Simpson immediately offered to take his place at Fort Wedderburn, a small post on an island in Lake Athabasca. There, he quickly learned about the fur trade and took steps to improve the discipline of the men in the smaller posts under his control.

Simpson soon experienced at first hand the bitter hostility of the Nor'Westers, whose Fort Chipewyan stood only a very short distance from Fort Wedderburn. Angered at their constant harassment, he forcibly arrested the leading Nor'Wester, Simon McGillivray. Although McGillivray escaped in the middle of the night back to Fort Chipewyan, Simpson had shown that he was capable of taking quick and firm action when necessary. He spent only one year in Athabasca. When he left the post in the spring to take his furs to York Factory, he learned that the two companies had united and that the long and bitter rivalry was over at last.

The new company, obviously impressed by his handling of affairs at Fort Wedderburn, appointed Simpson governor of the Northern Department. This gave authority over the vast area stretching from Hudson Bay to the Pacific coast to a man with only one year of experience in the fur trade. But his lack of experience was probably an advantage. He knew enough to understand the need for efficiency and decisive action, but he had not been involved long enough to make many enemies.

The officers of the new company first met at York Factory late in 1821, and Governor Simpson quickly showed his ability to overcome old hostilities. One trader who was present at that first meeting recalled many years later exactly what happened.

64

A portrait of Sir George Simpson in his later years. Although used to a rugged life, Simpson enjoyed formality and was conscious of the important position he held.

> This first social meeting of the superior officers . . . had some peculiar features, owing to the bitter feelings of the guests who had for many years been keen trade competitors, and sometimes personal antagonists in willing combat. The "proud Northwest bucks"—mostly Highlandmen—had been stalking about the old fort . . . not trying to converse with the Hudson's Bayites. It was "dollars to doughnuts"—as the saying is—whether the entertainment would be a "feed" or a "fight." Fortunately the governor in chief, Mr. (afterwards Sir George) Simpson . . . was present, endeavouring by courtesy and tact to complete his work . . . The two sections of the guests . . . kept wholly apart until the new governor moving in the throng with bows, smiles and introductions, brought about some conversation or handshaking between individuals . . .

It was appropriate that this meeting took place at York Factory. Now that the companies were united, the northern route through Hudson Bay and York Factory became the main supply route for the entire fur trade. The old Nor'Westers' route from Montreal through the Great Lakes was now used mainly for the express canoes which carried passengers and mail. With this change, Fort William lost much of its importance and soon became just another trading post.

The new governor of the Northern Department immediately set about making the business much more efficient. He focused first on Rupert's Land, where both former companies had built trading posts. Many of these he now closed. Then he reduced the number of employees by dismissing unsatisfactory or newly-joined servants and by offering pensions to encourage many senior men to retire. He tightened discipline by fining those who broke company rules and by dismissing promptly any servant guilty of serious misconduct.

Simpson stayed in Rupert's Land for nearly three years. Then, once he had reorganized and improved the trade there, he turned his attention to the lands west of the Rockies known as the Columbia District, where there was stiff competition from the Russians and the Americans. In 1824, convinced by what he had heard that trading was carried on very inefficiently there, he sent out a former Nor'Wester, the energetic John McLoughlin as chief factor. But Simpson could not rest until he had seen things for himself. Leaving York Factory three weeks after McLoughlin, he travelled so fast that he caught up with him, much to McLoughlin's annoyance!

When he reached Fort George on the Fraser River, Simpson immediately made some drastic changes: he retired unwanted employees with pensions, encouraged traders to grow more of their own food at the trading posts and reduced the prices paid to the Indians for their furs. After a short but hectic visit, he returned just as rapidly to Fort Garry.

Fast travel was typical of Simpson. For this he depended on his voyageurs, and he was never happier than when he was speeding along the countless waterways and sharing their hardships. Sometimes he announced his trips well in advance, but more often he just set off without prior warning. Many a trader kept on his toes through fear of one of his sudden unexpected visits. Everywhere he went, he was quick to reprimand laziness or bad behavior and was equally quick to spot ways to make the trading more profitable. He encouraged the use of new and quicker routes, and he introduced the sturdy York boats to replace the frail freight canoes.

As he sped between trading posts Simpson kept busy dictating notes to his secretary, who travelled with him, and making entries in his *Book of Servants' Characters*. This was the book in which he recorded what he really thought about the company employees—how efficient they were and what their good and bad qualities were. In case the book fell into the wrong hands, he identified his entries only by number. A separate sheet contained both names and numbers, so a person would have to have both book and sheet in order to decipher the contents.

Simpson was aware, too, of the need to find new supplies of furs and to safeguard existing ones. He therefore encouraged both exploration and careful conservation. When beaver or other fur-bearing animals were becoming scarce in an area, he recommended an end to trapping for several years until the number of animals had again increased. Only once did he oppose conservation. When he thought that the Americans would soon take

In October 1828, Governor Simpson and Chief Trader Archibald McDonald set out to discover whether or not it was true that the Fraser River could never be used as a trade route. They are seen here shooting the rapids above the present town of Yale, only one of the many times the travellers were in danger of being flung into the raging torrent. Simpson later wrote, "I should consider the passage down to be certain Death in nine attempts out of ten."

The spring brigade leaves Lachine, near Montreal, for the West. The warehouse stood across the Lachine canal from the Hudson's Bay Company headquarters. An express canoe is just moving out, and three freight canoes are being loaded on the far bank. After 1821 this route was only occasionally used for heavy freight, most of which went via York factory.

over large parts of the Oregon Territory, he suggested that the company strip it bare of furs before abandoning its posts.

Simpson's businesslike methods had soon impressed the London Committee, and when Governor Williams of the Southern Department retired in 1826, he was appointed to head both departments. In 1839, he became governor-in-chief. Altogether, Simpson ruled the Hudson's Bay Company with ruthless efficiency for nearly forty years. His domineering manner and his short stature earned him the appropriate nickname of "the Little Emperor." During these years the fur trade remained efficient and profitable. It also became more stable—trading procedures were well established and life in the fur-trade forts became more settled.

Hudson's Bay Company Trading Procedures

Trading procedures did not vary greatly from those used years before by the two rival companies, although they differed slightly from post to post. If the trader did not understand or trust the Indians with whom he was dealing, he would take extra precautions. When the Indians came to the fort, they first entered a waiting room with a connecting hallway into the trading room. They then went two at a time into the trading room with its stout protective barrier. Only when they had completed their trading and left were two more admitted.

But this was not the usual method. Once the two parties trusted each other, the trading was far more open and friendly. At the larger forts there was quite a ceremony when the Indians first arrived in spring with their furs. The senior company officer welcomed them. Then the Indian trading captain and his lieutenant were dressed in European clothes and escorted in procession to a special lodging place. Only after much ceremonial and exchanging of gifts did the actual trading start.

Trading was by barter and no money changed hands. The traders and Indians usually expressed the value of the trade goods and furs in terms of "whole beaver." This was the pelt of a perfect, full-grown beaver, killed in season, properly cured and weighing about half a kilogram. Nicholas Garry, a member of the London Committee, visited many of the forts in 1821 when he

Trading ceremony at York Factory in the 1780s. The arrival of the main body of Indians in the early summer was one of the most important events of the year. After being received by the fort's governor, the Indian chief and his lieutenant were dressed in European clothes and escorted with great pageantry to the chief's lodge.

came out to help organize the union of the two companies. He recorded in his diary some details of the values of furs and trade goods and how the trading took place:

> Beaver is the Standard to which all other skins are reduced and by which the Indians trade. For instance should an Indian have the following Skins:

Beaver, Whole or full grown	30 = 30	Whole Beaver
Beaver, Half or cub	11 = 5½	Whole Beaver
Otters, Prime, large	1 = 2	Whole Beaver
Otters, Prime, small	1 = 1	Whole Beaver
Fox, Black prime	1 = 2	Whole Beaver
Fox, Red	3 = 1½	Whole Beaver
Fox, White	4 = 2	Whole Beaver
Martins	9 = 3	Whole Beaver
	47	

> After the Trader has examined the Skins he tells the Indian his Trade amounts to 4 Tens and 7 mores at the same Time gives the Indian 47 quils, signifying that he will give him Goods. The Indian will perhaps take:

A Gun	=	11	Quils.
3 Yards Cloth	=	9	"
3 lb. of Powder	=	6	"
8 lb. of Shot	=	4	"
1 Large Blanket	=	8	"
1 Hatchet	=	2	"
1 File	=	1	"
1 3-Gallon Kettle	=	6	"
		47	

Neither side had a particular advantage in trading. The company had fixed rates of exchange as a guide to trading and the Indians were hard bargainers. Their trading captain would often stress the hardships they had suffered during the winter and then mix pleas for pity with thinly-veiled threats that if they did not get "good measure" they would go elsewhere with their furs. The company trader certainly did not have things all his own way.

The Life of the Trader

With the union of the two companies in 1821 and the reorganization which followed it, life in the larger fur-trading posts became much more settled. For over a century, fur traders living a lonely and

Until the mid 1800s very few Hudson's Bay Company men brought their white wives to the company's posts. An exception was Governor Henry Sergeant, who took command of Moose Fort on the southern shore of James Bay in 1683. Included in his party were his wife and her companion, who thus became the first white women to live in the Bay area.

isolated life in the remote forts had married Indian and Métis wives "after the custom of the country." This meant that although they had not been legally married by a clergyman, they lived together as man and wife. These were often very happy marriages, and Indian wives were also useful for the fur trade. They sometimes persuaded members of their tribe to bring more furs to the trader and they taught their husbands a lot about living in their harsh surroundings.

A few Indian and Métis wives, such as Amelia Douglas, rose to high positions in society. Born in 1812 to an Irish-Canadian father and a Cree mother, Amelia was noted for her beauty and quick intelligence. When her father became chief factor at Fort St. James in 1824, Amelia met and fell in love with a young clerk, James Douglas. They married when she was sixteen. As the ambitious James rose steadily in company ranks, Amelia helped and advised him. On one occasion she even saved his life through her quick action and her understanding of her Cree people. When James became governor of Vancouver Island and of British Columbia, Amelia took an active role in the life of the colonies, winning universal love and respect.

James and Amelia enjoyed a long and happy marriage, but others were not so fortunate. Problems often occurred when company men married Indian or Métis wives and then retired to live in eastern Canada or Britain. Sometimes when a trader moved to another post or left the West altogether, he simply abandoned his country wife and children and never saw them again; sometimes he left enough money to keep his family. But either way it was an unhappy situation, and it was only the rare trader who, like Douglas or like David Thompson, took his country wife and children with him when he moved on.

Governor Simpson, who had several country wives, began a new trend. On one of his visits to Britain he married his young cousin Frances and brought her out to live in Rupert's Land and later in Montreal. Other traders followed his example, and soon the major fur forts became settled little communities. York Factory was the most important because it was the main depot for the north. It was to York that the annual company ship came to bring supplies and take a cargo of furs back to Britain.

York Factory
The visitor to York Factory in the 1840s would probably have been discouraged at the first view of the fort from the sea. R. M. Ballantyne, who worked for the Hudson's Bay Company and later became world famous as a writer of adventure stories, once described York Factory as "a monstrous blot on a swampy spot with a partial view of the frozen sea." His description of the terrain was accurate. It was certainly a dreary and swampy spot. But the

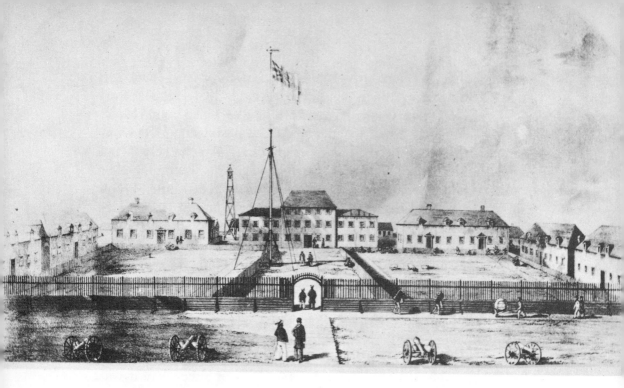

York Factory in the 1850s. This was the main depot for all western Canada after the union of the two companies in 1821. Company ships arriving here from Britain each year brought supplies and passengers and returned with the furs. York Factory lost much of its importancce with the development of overland trade routes between the Red River settlement and the United States in the 1860s.

fort itself was very impressive. It covered an area of two hectares and was surrounded by a sturdy wooden stockade. There were many fine buildings: a house for the chief factor; a large three-storey warehouse with two wings for visitors; a fur store; workshops for the various craftsmen; Bachelors' Hall, a residence for the clerks and apprentices; a provision store; and a powder magazine. In charge of the fort was the chief factor or the chief trader. Under him were all the people employed by the company. These formed two groups, the traders, clerks and apprentice clerks on the one hand, and the skilled artisans such as blacksmiths, boatbuilders, coopers and carpenters, and the laborers who helped in odd jobs around the fort on the other. Because of its importance, York Factory also had a postmaster and a doctor who looked after the company employees and the Indians who camped nearby.

The long winter at York Factory was a great hardship. But from the arrival of the first fur brigades in the spring to the departure of the company ship in the fall, life at York was hectic. Everything had to be done in a few short months: checking and repacking the furs brought by the inland brigades, and sorting and distributing the supplies brought from Britain. As York Factory was still the main port of entry to Rupert's Land, all visitors came through on their way to Red River and other inland posts. Social visits added to the already busy routines. There was always a sense of urgency. When the ship from Britain arrived in early June, the Captain, fearful of being caught by ice if he lingered at York, was forever hurrying things on so that he could get safely away in good time. With the departure of the supply ship and of the inland brigades, peace and quiet again descended for the winter.

Originally used to carry furs and freight between the Red River settlement and York Factory, these sturdy, flat-bottomed boats long remained in service on the lakes and bigger rivers. Although they varied in length and width depending on the waterway to be used, forty feet by ten feet amidships were the most common dimensions. They could carry loads of up to nine tonnes and often had crews of eleven.

Settlement in the West

While the company was doing well and making a good profit under the efficient control of Simpson, events were taking place which were bound to affect the fur trade sooner or later. Fur traders never really welcomed settlers, fearing that they would drive away the fur-bearing animals and eventually destroy the trade. Despite their opposition, however, settled colonies did gradually take root in the company's territories.

The first, and the most important, was Lord Selkirk's colony at Red River. Although Governor Simpson probably shared the fur traders' dislike of the farming settlement, he had to obey the orders of the London Committee, and it insisted that the colony must continue. Certainly it was a useful place for company men to live in retirement, and it might also be useful as a supply centre and a source of food. But it became a very troublesome problem.

Opposition to Company Rule

Simpson tried hard to strengthen the settlement, to improve its agriculture and industries, and to impose law and order. Red River gradually became a vigorous little community with a growing population of Scottish farmers, retired company officers and a large group of Métis. As time went on, many of these people began to resent the rule of the company. They wanted to be allowed to make money by trading for furs and by selling goods to the settlers. Both these practices were illegal because the company had a monopoly of trade. But could the company enforce the law? It had been easy enough to do so when all goods went through York Factory, but this was no longer the case. Now there was an overland trade route to St. Paul, Minnesota, and the company could not possibly control the increasing number of Red River carts which screeched across the open prairie to the United States.

The company soon realized that it was impossible to keep out retail stores which the settlers obviously wanted. Several stores opened and one merchant, it was said, could supply everything "with the exception of second-handed coffins." The company did try, however, to enforce its sole right to trade in furs. It got some help when British troops were stationed at Red River from 1846

The founding of Fort Victoria, 1843. Fort Vancouver on the Columbia River was for many years the headquarters of Hudson's Bay Company trade west of the Rockies. As American settlers began pouring into the area, however, the company realized that it would soon have to move. Chief Factor James Douglas chose a site at the southern end of Vancouver Island for a new depot, and company headquarters was moved in 1849, three years after the international boundary was established. Victoria is today the provincial capital of British Columbia.

to 1848, but when they left, it again became very difficult to enforce the law. The Métis did much of the illegal trading, and they were a well-organized and well-armed group. When a Métis named Sayer was charged with illegal trading and was taken before the court in 1849, a large crowd of his fellow Métis gathered outside. They were armed and ready to rescue him by force if things did not go well in the courtroom. In the end, the company did not dare to take any action although Sayer admitted his guilt. Anyone could now trade without fear of punishment.

The company also faced problems on the Pacific coast. There it did not actually own the land as it did at Red River, but it enjoyed a monopoly of trading rights. Chief Factor McLoughlin had welcomed American settlers moving into the Oregon Territory, and this eventually weakened the influence of the company. As the Americans grew stronger, they demanded that the whole territory become part of the United States. War was averted when the British and American governments reached a compromise: the international boundary at the forty-ninth parallel of latitude, agreed upon in 1818 as far west as the Rockies, was to be extended through the mountains to the Pacific coast. The company then moved its headquarters to Victoria on Vancouver Island. Here a settlement grew up and here, as in Red River, the settlers soon rebelled against company rule.

The End of Company Rule

By the early 1850s, the company had lost much of its power. Complaints from settlers at Red River reached London, where a committee of the British Parliament was discussing the company's rights. At these discussions, Governor Simpson ably defended the activities of the company and stoutly maintained that the lands in the West were highly unsuitable for settlement. But Simpson also recognized that times were changing and that the company would have to change too. As a result of the enquiry, Vancouver Island and later mainland British Columbia became colonies under direct British rule and the company lost its special trading rights. It was also decided that at some future date Rupert's Land would be taken over by Canada and opened up for settlement.

In 1869, just two years after Confederation, the company agreed to surrender Rupert's Land to Canada in return for a payment of £300,000. The company would keep its trading posts and the right to substantial blocks of land in the southern parts of what was to become the prairie provinces.

The transfer, however, was far from peaceful. It should have taken place on December 1, 1869, but by summer trouble was already brewing. Teams of surveyors from Canada arrived at Red River to prepare the way for the transfer of land. Unfortunately, no one knew they were coming, and they soon met armed resistance from the Métis, who feared that their lands would be stolen. Confusion followed, and the Métis leader, Louis Riel, seized power and formed a provisional government. After much discussion and some violence, delegates from Red River negotiated in Ottawa for the admission of the colony to Canada as a province. The settlement duly entered Canada as the province of Manitoba in 1870. The new province was only a small part of the lands known previously as Rupert's Land. The other lands became the Northwest Territories.

With the transfer complete, the shareholders of the Hudson's Bay Company were no longer "the true and absolute Lordes and Proprietors" of Rupert's Land. But the venerable company still dominated the fur trade. With a changed role, it now prepared to meet the future with the confidence born of long experience.

The Fur Trade Today

After the transfer of Rupert's Land in 1870, the Hudson's Bay Company kept its interest in the fur trade and in the North, but it now became more concerned with retail stores. Around the turn of the century, new organizations, such as that of Révillon Frères, began to compete for the fur trade in some areas. Révillon, a French firm with a long and distinguished history as furriers, decided in 1901 to establish its own trading posts in Canada. It began with five posts on James Bay and rapidly expanded its operations until by 1923 it had about forty-seven posts from Labrador to British Columbia. In the mid 1920s, however, its business began to decline, and in 1936 it sold its Canadian trading operations to the Hudson's Bay Company.

During the twentieth century, the Hudson's Bay Company gradually came more and more under Canadian control, until in 1970, three hundred years after the granting of the royal charter by Charles II, company headquarters moved from London to Winnipeg. Today, the Hudson's Bay Company is a thriving retail chain whose large department stores in all major Canadian cities contrast vividly with its scores of isolated posts in remote communities throughout the North.

The fur trade, which built the Hudson's Bay Company, still thrives today, but it has had its ups and downs in the last century. Demand for furs remained fairly steady until the outbreak of the First World War, but afterwards prices fluctuated. They rose sharply in the 1920s, but then declined equally sharply a few years later, leaving many trappers without a livelihood. These changes

Governor General Roland Michener signed the new Canadian charter of the Hudson's Bay Company in 1970. This transferred the company headquarters from England to Canada.

occur because the fur business depends on so many things over which it has no control. The main demand for furs is for women's fashions, and they can change with little warning. One year fur may be fashionable; another year it may not. One year mink is fashionable; the next year fox may be preferred.

Furs are also a status symbol. This means that some people buy and wear expensive furs not only to keep warm or because they like them, but also to impress other people. Demand for furs, of course, also depends on prices; and prices often depend on demand. In times of depression the demand for furs usually decreases sharply; in times of war it virtually ceases.

In the 1970s, the fur trade had some of its best years. The

United States, Japan and many European countries were enjoying prosperous times. Many people had money to spend on luxury goods and the demand for furs rose rapidly. Prices also rose for nearly all kinds of furs. Even the coyote's pelt, which brought the trapper $3 in the early 1960s, brought as much as $100 in the late 1970s while a top-quality pelt might sell for as much as $200.

For many years the mink coat was the recognized status symbol. Now mink has given way to red squirrel and to longhair furs such as fox, lynx, badger and wolf. Of these, the lynx pelt, averaging over $500, is the most expensive. But fashions keep on changing. Once a particular fur becomes too popular or drops in price, fashionable people switch to more expensive furs. Beaver, the fur that really started the fur trade three hundred years ago, is still the best-wearing fur in all the world, but it has been almost forgotten by Canadians. Beaver coats sell well in the United States, Japan and Europe, but not in Canada.

Supplies of some furs can quite easily be controlled. Mink, rabbit and blue and silver fox, for example, are raised on fur farms, where numbers can be regulated. But there are only limited numbers of those animals that are caught in the wild. Fur traders, therefore, have long recognized the importance of conservation.

If hunters or trappers kill as many animals as they like, they run the risk of killing them all. Hunting and trapping, like fishing, has to be controlled. This gives the animals the chance to breed and to restore their numbers. In Canada there are several ways of controlling the killing of animals. Each province licenses trappers who have to pay a fee for permission to trap in a certain area. The number of animals they can trap is carefully regulated, and certain animals can be taken only between fixed dates. The time allowed, known as the open season, varies from area to area and depends mainly on the type of animal. For example, the trapping of foxes and lynx, whose fur remains prime for a comparatively short period, may be allowed for only the three coldest months of the year. Other animals, such as mink, otter, beaver and muskrat, are more or less amphibious and their fur remains in prime condition for a longer time. Their open season is therefore longer than that for foxes or lynx. As a means of conservation, however, the length of the open season can be changed according to the estimated supply of each fur-bearing species.

The fur industry is still very valuable. It brings in millions of dollars from sales to other countries, and it employs thousands of people within Canada. Probably as many as seventy-five thousand people, some of them part-time, have trap lines on private property or registered trap lines on crown lands.

When a trapper in northern Ontario or Manitoba completes his catch for the winter, this is only the first of many steps before the fur becomes part of a fashionable coat. The trapper first takes his pelts to a northern fur trader. The trader then ships them to a fur auction in cities such as Winnipeg, Montreal or North Bay, Ontario. For many years, the Hudson's Bay Company dominated all fur sales in Canada, but recently the sales at North Bay, organized by the Ontario Trappers' Association, have increased tremendously. Ontario is the world's richest fur-producing region, and 60 percent of its furs are now sold at North Bay. The Hudson's Bay Company still dominates the sales of wild furs at Winnipeg and of ranch-raised furs at Montreal. The total value of all furs sold at auction in 1979 was over $70 million.

Furs sold at auction are usually bought by middlemen known as brokers. These brokers in turn sell them to customers in different parts of the world. It is these customers who actually make the fur coats for sale to the public. And there is still a great demand for them. Canadians alone spend over $500 million each year for manufactured furs!

The fur trade, despite its long history, still has its problems. Just as important as problems of changing fashions and varying prices is the question of how the public sees the fur trade. The main criticism has always been that furs are a luxury that cause unnecessary suffering to animals. Furs, of course, are a luxury. They are warm and they are fashionable, but they are not absolutely necessary. This is even truer today, when there are so many alternatives available, such as nylon made to look like fur and lightweight coats filled with down. Yet people still buy fur coats because they are fashionable; and for every fur coat that is made, several animals have to die. It seems strange that people who treat their dogs and cats like humans will ignore the deaths of countless other animals when they buy their fur coats.

The event which raises most protest is undoubtedly the annual seal hunt off the coast of Labrador. There, each spring, hunters from several nations pursue the herds of harp seals on the ice floes and kill the newly-born seal pups. Despite the protests, however, the killing of these and other fur-bearing animals will continue as long as the demand for furs persists.

The fur trade has played a unique role in Canadian history. The discovery of furs led first to French settlement and then to English. Competition for furs heightened the later conflicts between the two nations and led ultimately to the exploration of the farthest reaches of the country. At the same time, the involvement of the native Indians as partners both in trade and in exploration changed forever their way of life and posed problems which have still to be resolved.

Over four hundred years have now passed since Cartier and the Indians bartered for furs on the banks of the St. Lawrence. Little could they have realized that they were laying the foundation of Canada as we know it today.

Selected Biographies

CHAMPLAIN, Samuel de (1567?-1635)
Champlain was born in Brouage, France, and took to the sea at an early age. In 1603 he took part in a fur-trading voyage to the St. Lawrence and mapped much of the shore line. In the following year he joined the expedition to Acadia where he remained until the Port Royal settlement was abandoned in 1607. His greatest achievement was the founding of Quebec in 1608. Between 1609 and 1616, he undertook several voyages of exploration, first south to Lake Champlain, then northwest to Georgian Bay and from there down to the region south of Lake Ontario. Forced to surrender Quebec temporarily to the English from 1629 to 1632, Champlain was again placed in command in 1633 and successfully rebuilt the settlement. It was there that he died two and a half years later. He is popularly known as the "Father of New France."

FRASER, Simon (1776-1862)
Simon Fraser was born in what is now the State of Vermont just before the outbreak of the American Revolution. His loyalist father died in prison, and after the war his mother brought him to Canada where they settled near Cornwall. Educated at Montreal, Fraser became an apprentice in the North West Company in 1792. He worked mainly in the Athabasca region until he was placed in charge of company operations beyond the Rocky Mountains in 1805.

Over the next three years, Fraser explored the area and built a number of trading posts, the first in what is now British Columbia. Then in 1808, he undertook the journey that made him famous, the exploration of the Fraser River to its mouth on the Pacific coast. In 1816, Fraser was among those arrested by Lord Selkirk and accused of involvement in the tragic incident at Seven Oaks. He was tried in 1818 and acquitted. By then he had retired to a farm in Upper Canada, where he engaged rather unsuccessfully in various business enterprises. A knee injury received while serving in the militia during the 1837 rebellion handicapped him severely, and he spent his last years in relative poverty.

GROSEILLIERS, Médard Chouart, Sieur des (1618-1696?)
Groseilliers came to Canada from France in 1642 to work with the Jesuit missions to the Hurons, but he soon took to fur trading. Between 1654 and 1656, he reached Lake Michigan on a highly successful trading expedition that reopened the western fur trade, which had been closed by the Iroquois. He made a second westward journey in 1659-60 with his brother-in-law,

Pierre Esprit Radisson. They reached the southern shore of Lake Superior, collected a rich load of furs and became convinced of the possibility of a water route to Hudson Bay. Angered by their treatment at the hands of the governor of New France, who fined them for trading without a licence. Groseilliers offered his services to the English. With Radisson, he convinced them of the potential value of Hudson Bay for furs. This led to the formation of the Hudson's Bay Company.

In 1676 Groseilliers returned to the service of the French and established Fort Bourbon at the mouth of the Hayes River. It later passed into English hands and became York Factory. Little is known about Groseilliers' later life.

HEARNE, Samuel (1745-1792)

Born in London, England, Samuel Hearne joined the Royal Navy at the age of eleven and served in it until 1763. Three years later he joined the Hudson's Bay Company and was sent to Fort Prince of Wales at the mouth of the Churchill River. After three years on company ships, he was put in charge of inland exploration. He made several attempts to explore the Coppermine River, and finally in 1771 he became the first man to reach the Arctic Ocean overland. In 1774 he built Cumberland House, the first inland post of the Hudson's Bay Company. He was appointed governor of Fort Prince of Wales in 1775, but was forced to surrender it to the French in 1782. A year later he established a new post named Fort Churchill at the site. In 1787 he retired to England where he spent his last years writing an account of his journeys which is remarkable for its skilled observation and realism.

KELSEY, Henry (c. 1667-1724)

A native of London, England, Henry Kelsey joined the Hudson's Bay Company as an apprentice in 1684. For the next thirty-eight years he played a part in almost all the major events at Hudson Bay. In 1690-92 he made a remarkable journey inland in an effort to persuade the Indians to the south to bring their furs to the posts on the Bay. Travelling with the Indians, Kelsey probably reached The Pas on the Saskatchewan River in present-day Manitoba. He thus became the first white man to see the prairies and the great herds of buffalo. He also acquired a rare knowledge of Indian languages.

Captured by d'Iberville at York Factory in 1694, Kelsey was imprisoned in France. A little over a year later he returned to York Factory, where he was captured a second time in 1697. He subsequently held commands at various posts on the Bay until his retirement in 1722.

LA VERENDRYE, Pierre Gaultier de Varennes, Sieur de (1685-1749)

La Vérendrye, who was born at Trois-Rivières, served several years in the

French army and saw action in the American colonies, in Newfoundland and in Europe. On returning to New France, he became a successful fur trader. Intrigued by Indian tales of a "western sea," he began to make plans to go in search of it. With his sons and a nephew, he set out in 1731. Over the next few years, they explored far to the west and built a chain of fur-trading forts.

Although he failed to reach the western sea, La Vérendrye's explorations did much to establish French power in the West and to threaten the dominance of the Hudson's Bay Company. His accomplishment was not immediately appreciated by the government or by the merchants who had helped finance him, and in 1743 he was virtually forced to give up command of the western posts. He returned to Montreal, where the value of his services was eventually recognized. In 1749 he began planning another expedition to the West but died before he could leave Montreal.

MACKENZIE, Sir Alexander (1764-1820)
Alexander Mackenzie's family emigrated from Scotland to New York in 1774. At the outbreak of the American Revolution two years later, young Mackenzie was sent north to school in Montreal. At the age of fifteen he went to work for a small trading company which was later absorbed by the North West Company. Mackenzie soon became a partner in the larger firm, and in 1788 he was placed in charge of the Athabasca region. The following year, he set out from Fort Chipewyan on the first of his major explorations and reached the Arctic Ocean by the river system now known by his name. His journey to the Pacific Ocean four years later established him as one of Canada's greatest explorers.

Mackenzie left the North West Company in 1799 and returned to Britain, where he published his memoirs and was knighted in 1802. Back in Canada, he became the leading partner of the XY Company, but ceased to take any active role in the fur trade when it merged with the North West Company. After sitting in the legislature of Lower Canada from 1804 to 1808, Mackenzie left Canada for good and retired to Scotland.

POND, Peter (1740-1807)
Born in Connecticut in what is now the United States, Peter Pond served as a soldier before becoming a fur trader. He came northwest in 1775 and established the first trading post in Athabasca three years later.

Pond could scarcely read or write, but was skilled at living off the country. He was the first white man to take trade goods to the Chipewyans, who introduced him to pemmican. A skilled trader, he became interested in exploration and soon got to know the waterways of the Northwest. He carefully mapped many of these, and his enthusiasm encouraged Mackenzie to persevere in his own explorations. Pond was an initial partner in the North West Company, but was obliged to withdraw after his involvement in two murders. He retired to the United States, where he died poor and forgotten.

RADISSON, Pierre Esprit (1636?-1710)

All that is known for certain of Radisson's early life is that he was born in France and that in 1651 he was living with his half-sister in Trois-Rivières. In the following year he was captured by the Iroquois but managed to escape after about two years. He again spent some time in Iroquois country in 1657-58 when he accompanied a group of Jesuits to a mission that had been established there. There is little doubt that it was his understanding of the Iroquois language and mentality that saved the missionaries when the Iroquois turned against them.

In 1660 Radisson joined his brother-in-law, Groseilliers, in exploring the country west of the Great Lakes. Both later offered their services to the King of England and were influential in events leading to the formation of the Hudson's Bay Company in 1670. In 1676 Radisson rejoined the French, but in 1684 he again changed his allegiance and re-entered the service of the English company, with which he remained until his death. A flamboyant man with a flair for drama and exaggeration, he was probably responsible for attracting the interest and support of Charles II for the Hudson's Bay Company.

SELKIRK, Thomas Douglas, 5th earl of (1771-1820)

A Scottish nobleman and philanthropist, Thomas Douglas succeeded to the earldom of Selkirk and a considerable fortune in 1799. Wishing to relieve the distress of crofters evicted from the Scottish highlands, Selkirk planned colonies for them in Prince Edward Island and in Upper Canada. His main project, however, was the Red River colony established on land granted by the Hudson's Bay Company, of which he had secured financial control. The first of several parties of settlers arrived in 1812. In 1816, the North West Company's opposition to the settlement led to the battle of Seven Oaks, the death of the colony's governor and the temporary dispersal of the settlers. Selkirk seized Fort William and arrested several leading Nor'Westers in retaliation, and then re-established the colony at Red River on a firm basis. There followed a series of legal battles between Selkirk and the North West Company, and Selkirk came out the loser. Broken in health, he returned to England and later died in southern France.

SIMPSON, Sir George (1787?-1860)

Raised in the barren north of Scotland, Simpson left school at the age of fourteen to work as a clerk in a London counting house. Family connections secured him a job with the Hudson's Bay Company, and in 1820 he took charge of the remote Fort Wedderburn at Lake Athabasca. He soon mastered the intricacies of the fur trade and showed the bold and ruthless characteristics that later stood him in good stead. After only a year in the fur trade, Simpson became governor of the Northern Department. Five years later, he was put in charge of the Southern Department as well, and he controlled the fur trade virtually single-handedly from then until his death. He became governor-in-chief of the company in 1839 and was knighted two years later.

Simpson was a businessman—efficient, ruthless, sometimes unfair; but his capacity for kindness won him considerable loyalty. He, in turn, was loyal to the company directors even when he disagreed with their policies. His death coincided with the decline of the fur trade and of the fortunes of the Hudson's Bay Company. His short stature and domineering ways earned him the nickname of "the Little Emperor."

THOMPSON, David (1770-1857)

Born and educated in London, England, David Thompson was apprenticed to the Hudson's Bay Company and sent to Fort Churchill at the age of fourteen. For thirteen years he worked as a clerk at various posts, did some exploring and studied surveying. In 1797 he transferred to the rival North West Company, in which he became a partner. From then until 1812, Thompson was busy in the fur trade and in explorations of the northwest and Pacific-coast regions. He was the first white man to travel the full length of the Columbia River. The accurate maps he made of the land he travelled through served as the basis for all later cartography. Moving to eastern Canada in 1812, Thompson was later employed in surveying the international boundary with the United States. He died in poverty at Longueuil near Montreal.

Glossary

Canot de maître   Also known as a "Montreal canoe," this was a large freight canoe used mainly on the route from Montreal to Fort William. About thirteen metres in length, the canot de maître could carry four or five tonnes of cargo and had a crew of about twelve.

Canot du nord   The "North canoe" was a smaller birchbark canoe used mainly on the rivers and smaller lakes to the north and west of Lake Superior. Up to ten metres long, it could carry nearly two tonnes of cargo, a crew of eight or nine and two or three passengers.

Charter   A written document, usually issued by a king, granting certain privileges or possessions to an individual or group.

Coureur de bois   "Runner of the woods," an independent trader who ranged the forests in search of furs. When the government of New France made it illegal to trade in furs without a government-issued license, the term came to refer to those who went out without one in defiance of the law.

Factory   A fur-trading post, especially one of the larger transshipment depots where large quantities of food and supplies were stored.

Métis   A person of mixed Indian and European ancestry. At one time the term was used only for those of mixed Indian and French blood, but it is now used generally to describe all "mixed blood" people.

Monopoly   The sole right to trade in particular goods. If a company had a monopoly of the fur trade in a certain place, for example, only that company could legally trade in furs in that area. If the company had no competitors, it could raise prices to make as much profit as possible.

Portage   Canoes and boats, along with their cargo, often had to be carried from one lake or river to another or around rapids or falls. *Portage* was used to describe the places where this happened (for instance, Methye Portage) or the act of doing it (as in, "we had to make a portage").

Shareholder   Companies like the Hudson's Bay Company had to have money to operate and they raised it by selling shares. The people who bought the shares were called shareholders, and they participated in the profits of the company in proportion to the number of shares they owned.

Voyageur   A canoeman or boatman, usually a French Canadian, Orkneyman, Indian or Métis, who manned the vessels of the inland fur trade.

Selected Further Reading

Andrews, R.J. *The Fur Fort.* Toronto: Ginn and Company, 1970. A well-illustrated account of the role of the forts in the fur trade, with details of construction, location and of the trading ceremonies.

The Voyageurs. Toronto: Ginn and Company, 1969. The story of the voyageurs, their hardships and their achievements.

The Beaver. Winnipeg: Hudson's Bay House. A quarterly magazine about the part of Canada that was once controlled by the Hudson's Bay Company.

Campbell, Marjorie Wilkins. *The Fur Trade.* (Jackdaw Kit C5). Toronto: Clarke, Irwin, 1971. An interesting kit containing extensive notes, pictures and facsimiles of documents.

The Nor'Westers. Toronto: Macmillan, 1973. A detailed account of the North West Company from its beginnings until it merged with the Hudson's Bay Company in 1821.

The Savage River. Toronto: Macmillan, 1968. A well-told account of Simon Fraser's journey from Fort George to the Pacific in 1808.

Healy, W.J. *Women of Red River.* Winnipeg: Peguis, 1967. Recollections, first published in 1923, of the women of the Red River Settlement.

The Manitoba Trappers' Guide. Winnipeg: Department of Mines, Natural Resources and Environment, 1979. Details of trapping methods and regulations

Morse, Eric W. *Fur Trade Canoe Routes of Canada/Then and Now.* Toronto: University of Toronto Press, 1979. A thorough account of the canoe routes and the problems they presented, based on first-hand experience.

Neering, Rosemary. *Fur Trade.* Toronto: Fitzhenry & Whiteside, 1974. A straight-forward account of the fur trade for younger readers.

Wilson, Clifford. *Adventurers from the Bay.* Toronto: Macmillan, 1962. An account of the men of the Hudson's Bay Company and their work in what is now western Canada.

Wilson, Keith. *George Simpson and the Hudson's Bay Company.* Agincourt: Book Society of Canada, 1977. The colorful career of Simpson is set in the context of the rise and gradual decline of the fur trade. Profusely illustrated and with suggested activities for students.

Life at Red River: 1830-1860. Toronto: Ginn and Company, 1970. A well-illustrated account of various aspects of social life at the Red River settlement.

For Discussion

THE BEAVER

1) Why were furs so widely used during the Middle Ages?
2) Why and how do beavers build dams?
3) Explain what is meant by conservation and why it is important.
4) Find out whether the population of beavers is increasing or decreasing today.

BEGINNINGS AND NEW FRANCE

1) Find a map of the world as imagined before the voyages of Columbus and compare it with today's map. What differences are there? Are there still parts of the world unmapped?
2) Read the poem "Jacques Cartier" by Thomas D'Arcy McGee.
3) Why was fish so important to Europeans in the sixteenth century?
4) Place-names often reflect history. Choose five places near you and find out how they got their names.
5) If you were building a habitation, where and how would you build it?
6) What were the main dangers faced by the early inhabitants of Quebec?
7) What were the main arguments for and against the granting of a fur-trade monopoly in New France?
8) The granting of seigniories was really a continuation of the feudal system. Find out what is meant by *feudal* and how land was owned and farmed in the Middle Ages.
9) Why did the French government want to strengthen the colony at Quebec?
10) Look at a historical atlas and find out which Indian tribes lived near the St. Lawrence River and the Great Lakes.
11) If you were a young coureur de bois living among the Hurons, how would you learn their language?
12) Why did the Roman Catholic church want to convert the Indians to Christianity?
13) Find out more about the religious beliefs of the Indians.
14) What were the main problems faced by New France in 1663 just before the imposition of royal government?

RIVALS FOR THE TRADE

1) Groseilliers reported finding a lake as large as the Caspian Sea. Using an atlas, find the fifteen largest lakes in the world.
2) When traders penetrated into unknown lands, they often had to shoot wild animals and fowl in order to survive. What animals would they have found in the Great Lakes region?
3) Marie de l'Incarnation founded the Ursuline convent in Quebec. What is a convent? What did the Ursuline Sisters do in the young colony?
4) What would be the main problems faced by ships sailing from England to Hudson Bay?
5) What is an auction? Find out how auctions were conducted in the 1660s.
6) Consult a historical atlas and find the largest extent of French rule in North America.
7) On a map trace the journeys made by La Vérendrye and his sons. What were their main problems?
8) In what ways were the British stronger than the French in North America before 1760?

TWO GREAT COMPANIES

1) If the Hudson's Bay Company owned Rupert's Land, why were other fur traders allowed to operate there?
2) In the rivalry between the Hudson's Bay Company and the North West Company, what advantages and disadvantages did each side have?
3) Why was Fort William such an important post for the North West Company?
4) Voyageurs faced many hardships and dangers, and yet there were always plenty of men willing to become voyageurs. Why would men want to take so hard a job? What do you imagine their wives thought of their way of life?
5) Learn the words and music to one popular voyageur song.
6) On a map trace the two main explorations of Alexander Mackenzie.
7) What were the most valuable furs in the Pacific coast area of British Columbia?
8) Read more about the founding and early history of the settlement at Red River.
9) Imagine that you are one of the women in the first party of Selkirk settlers. Write a letter to your sister in Scotland describing your new home and some of your activities in summer and winter. You might like to refer to W.J. Healy's book, *Women of Red River*.

THE NEW HUDSON'S BAY COMPANY

1) Look at a map showing the fur-trading districts. Can you tell why the districts were established in this way?
2) Why do you think Governor Simpson was called "the Little Emperor"?
3) Would you like to have been a trader under the rule of Simpson? Explain your reasons.
4) Was Simpson a good choice as governor of the Hudson's Bay Company?
5) Fort Frances, Ontario, was named in honor of Frances Simpson, the wife of Governor Simpson. Can you find any places in Canada named after fur traders or voyageurs?
6) Imagine that you are a young clerk at York Factory. Write a letter to your parents in Scotland describing your experiences during your first summer at York.
7) James Douglas is called the "Father of British Columbia." Find out why.
8) How did Métis and Indian wives like Amelia Douglas help their husbands in the fur trade?

THE FUR TRADE TODAY

1) Talk to three people who own fur coats. Ask them what kind of fur they are and why they bought them.
2) Find out more about fur farms. For example, what animals are raised, what the animals are fed, what are some of the difficulties in raising fur-bearing animals.
3) Arrange a class debate on the motion . . . "That the trapping of animals is cruel and should be banned".

Index